What Scientists Actually Do

Joan
Horvath

ILLUSTRATIONS BY
Nichole S. Wong

WITH A FOREWORD BY
Greg Bear

STARRAZER
Publishing Company
PO Box 77002
Corona, CA 92877-0100
"Educate, Enlighten, Entertain"

Published by Stargazer Publishing Company
PO Box 77002   (800) 606-7895
Corona, CA 92877-0100   (951) 898-4619
www.stargazerpub.com   FAX: (951) 898-4633
Corporate e-mail: stargazer@stargazerpub.com
Orders e-mail: orders@stargazerpub.com

Edited by Hope Frazier and Doug Adrianson
Illustrations by Nichole S. Wong. Overall cover design by Beatrice
Aispuro, Joan Horvath and Steven Montgomery, incorporating art by
Nichole S. Wong.

ISBN: 978-1-933277-08-0

LCCN: 2007927411

Publisher's Cataloging-in-Publication
(Provided by Quality Books, Inc.)

Horvath, Joan C.
    What scientists actually do / Joan Horvath ;
illustrations by Nichole Wong ; foreword by Greg Bear.
    p. cm.
    LCCN 2007927411
    ISBN-13: 978-1-933277-08-0
    ISBN-10: 1-933277-08-4

    1. Science--Popular works. 2. Science--Methodology--
Popular works. 3. Scientists--Popular works.
I. Wong, Nichole, ill. II. Title.

Q162.H64 2008   500
                        QBI07-600159

Dedication

To the first human being who successfully talked a friend through the process of creating fire.

iv

Table of Contents

Foreword and Preface

Foreword
by Greg Bear

One way or another, my whole life is wrapped up in science. Or, more broadly speaking, it's wrapped up in getting to know things: new things, old things. But knowledge. As far as I'm concerned, everything I know is open to question – I've been wrong so many times! And so, learning is not about absolutes. It's about *change.*

At an early age, I began my (sort of) scientific career by messing around with Erector Sets, model kits, wooden blocks. I filled kitchens and bedrooms with cityscapes made of stacked blocks – mighty ceiling-scrapers taller than I was, perfectly balanced.

My parents were both readers, both naturally curious, and my father – a meteorologist in the U.S. Navy – often worked with such technological marvels as high-altitude balloons and *computers*, still new in the 1960s. Travel around the Far East and the United States introduced me to strange climates, unusual insects (biting ants, walking sticks) – and some minor tropical diseases. It was all grist for my very young mill, and so I ground up what I knew – and messed around with chemistry sets, Mobius strips (page 49), Heathkits, whatever was available – and in the '60s, post-Sputnik, a *lot* was available. The United States felt it needed to catch up with the Soviet Union, which had just launched the first orbiting satellite and put the first human being in space. It was a terrific, scary time – hydrogen bombs and Cold War nightmares, real rockets lifting off (or not) on national television, and science fiction – wow! Lots of science fiction magazines and paperbacks and science books available in grocery stores, liquor stores, drugstores – people were *reading* everything, everywhere.

I studied fibers and mold spores and mosquito larvae under a nice toy microscope that I still have. Somehow, I made blue gelatinous substances in test tubes, and bent glass pipes over an alcohol burner for laboratory equipment – then skewered my thumb as I tried to push one through a rubber cork! But that didn't stop me.

The United States – possibly much of the world – had never been more curious and full of ideas and big questions than it was in the 1960s.

Now, we live in the golden glow of all the pioneers who came out of the troubled 19th and 20th centuries and studied and wrote and built great things. We're still learning and building great things, and science is moving forward faster than ever – but the rate of *applications*, the actual rate of change, has slowed on many fronts. Notable exceptions are biology and electronics,

particularly computers. And possibly mathematics –
with the help of those omnipresent computers.

Airplanes look much the way they did in the 1960s,
though they are faster, better, lighter – and much more
expensive. Consider the advances in airplane design
between 1914 and 1959, 45 years – from wood-and-
fabric biplane to SR-71. There's been nothing like that
extreme scale of change in airframe design in the
decades since. No flying cars – no jetpacks – no piloted
mission to Mars, no time travel, and, for that matter, we
have yet to get back to the moon, *40 years later!*

But none of that has stopped me from hoping for
better things in my lifetime, learning – or imagining –
how things will be different in the future. Though many
of the obvious changes may seem to arrive more slow-
ly, the knowledge being gathered seems to shoot
straight out of a thrashing, high-pressure fire hose.
Keeping up with the stream of scientific facts is
impossible for a single individual – and has been for a
long time.

But making theories – playing around with new
facts – coming up with new ways to synthesize those
facts into larger schemes of understanding – plenty of
room left for everybody to join in.

I'm not a scientist, but I constantly study and sometimes even *do* science, just for fun. A few years ago, I
rigged up a medical-grade microscope with a home

video camera – removing the microscope objective and simply aiming the camera lens down the tube, then focusing until the image was sharp. I hooked the camera to a TV and showed off tiny creatures living in our nearby lake to writers attending a local workshop. Mr. Wizard, Bill Nye wannabe? Absolutely.

I still love to swap information and ideas with working scientists. It's a great way to get ideas for stories, and then make those ideas plausible – or at least *more* plausible.

Once you hook up to the thrashing fire hose, it's like riding a tiger – you can't let go, can't get off, and the ride is so much fun maybe you don't want to. Science is the greatest game of all. Your opponent – your adversary, your trickster, your teacher, your greatest friend – is the entire Universe.

Joan Horvath admirably captures that spirit in this wonderful book. Dip in. Look around. Figure it out.

Have fun!

April 6, 2007

Greg Bear is the award-winning author of more than 30 books of science fiction and fantasy.

Preface

If you are reading this book, presumably you want, or need, to know something about science. Perhaps you are a third-grade teacher who has not taken a science class in 30 years ... but you have to teach science for the first time *tomorrow*. Or, a scientist or engineer friend has handed this book to you after you've asked one time too many, "What do you *do* all day?" Maybe you are a high school or college student trying to decide if you want a technology career. Or you are a reasonably well-informed voter wondering how issues like evolution and global warming can still be considered controversial in this day and age.

In any case, suppose you need to learn all about science by tomorrow morning and it is now 8 p.m. Learning science takes time and there is no way you can learn how to be a scientist overnight. However, this book is intended to give you a fast sweep of science as a whole and its context in the world. How do scientists who study very big systems – like the Earth – develop their ideas and test them out? If scientists have some uncertainty about what they know, is that OK? How do you decide what to believe about what you read in the newspaper or see on television?

In this short book, you will not learn how to *be* a scientist, but you will learn what scientists working in a broad spectrum of areas consider to be the core values of how they do their work and how they see it fitting into society. No one really studies all of "science." Most scientists work a specific field like chemistry or biology, but they have to maintain a big picture about how their specialty fits into the world. Most of the concepts in the book are explained from personal, "here's how I think about it" points of view of scientists, engineers and mathematicians.

You should also know what this book is *not*. It is not a set of recipes for science fair experiments, nor is it directly intended for children. It does not replace the need to study science in depth (which, if I have succeeded, you might want to do after reading this book!).

I thought it was important for readers to start their journey by seeing how people become scientists. The stories in Section 1 may surprise you (and perhaps remind you a bit of your own career choices). Section 2 explores how science differs in some key ways from its portrayal in science fiction. The core of the book is Section 3, which covers how scientists develop ideas. If you can't read the whole book, be sure to read this section! Sections 4 and 5 introduce you to scientists in different fields to give you some sense of the broad range of science careers – while showing how a spirit of exploration drives them all. Section 6 offers some guidance about how to interpret science in the media, and Section 7 examines how you might think about choices you make that involve science issues.

This book has been a team effort with many talented individuals expending incredible amounts of time and energy. First of all, editors Hope Frazier and Doug Adrianson helped frame this book, and subsequently pounded sense into it by asking hard questions (and refusing to go away when I told them to stop!). I feel like I've taken a high-speed course in journalism – and journalistic ethics – from some of the best in the business. The interviewees who answered my off-the-wall questions with good humor and great insight made abstract concepts come to life.

Artist Nichole Wong's *Bob* and *Betty* characters, as we've come to affectionately call them, have been an inspiration as they took shape and developed personalities. I am also grateful to Greg Bear for supplying such a fine Foreword. Stargazer Publishing Company has my thanks for taking on this book and weathering the fits and starts in its preparation. The tactful souls who read early versions, notably Stephen Unwin, Peggy Risinger and many of the scientists featured on these pages all gave thoughtful comments that smoothed out some of the bumps. Any remaining "huh?" moments in the book are my fault!

More personally, I would like to thank all the people who taught me to be an engineer and to appreciate the wonder of discovering the natural world. From my parents, through the many formal and informal teachers I've had, to my astronomer husband Stephen Unwin, there has always been someone to teach me something new and amazing. I hope I can do the same for you in the pages of this book!

Joan Horvath
Pasadena, California
May 2007

Section 1

Becoming a Scientist

Beginnings

Y ou can never be sure if a fuzzy memory from early childhood really happened, or if you've just been told the story so many times that you fluffed it out from family legend. You might start with a vague snippet, and add a detail here and there, as newer remembrances leak into and color older ones. The first seed of a lifetime passion or goal is particularly that way – a memory revisited so many times that it is rubbed to gleaming, like a genie's lamp.

Mine involves the innards of an early-1960s television: A failed television, fixable with a dab dropped *just so* from a soldering iron. I have a soldering iron in my seven- or eight-year-old hand front and center, framed by my blonde pigtails. Dad the electrician says in his Brooklyn accent, punctuated with a jabbing finger, "See that busted wire? That's your problem, *right there*." With Mom worrying that my hair will catch on fire from the soldering iron, a blobby silver bit goes from solder wire to TV. The broken connection now whole, the iron goes back into its curled wire holder. The TV guts with my solder job returns to its cabinet, and *works*....

Growing up in the rocket-fueled 1960s, it seemed like everyone wanted to be an astronaut. I certainly did, a short blonde kid in 6A of a New York City apartment building. My favorite show, *Star Trek,* was in its first run, and the TV had to be in top working order to keep up with Kirk and Spock. I did my homework suspended six floors up, maybe one-fifth as high off the ground as my heroes sitting on top of Apollo 11's Saturn V. In those days, aspiring to be a scientist or engineer (particularly a "rocket scientist") was like the call to the priesthood was in medieval Europe. You would learn the mysteries, and save the populace from the Russkies. It never occurred to me to wonder whether "girls" did these things – I was a scientist in my head from about age seven, and being a girl was pretty much irrelevant one way or the other. I was much more worried about needing to wear glasses, since everyone knew astronauts needed perfect vision!

Becoming a scientist or engineer is hard. For six years of undergraduate and graduate school, during the term it was rare to study less than 12 to 16 hours a day, six or seven days a week. Given that, why do people become scientists? Common wisdom would say that a teacher, a mentor or a role model drives the decision. Certainly, that can be true. Yet many of us remember an incident: a puzzle being solved, figuring out how something worked, some time we had to expend most of our creativity to keep our authority figures from discovering the aftermath of our first experiments! It's the chase that takes us through it, the feeling that there are greater and greater things to fix and to solve out there – if only we learn, say, one or two more ways that magnetic fields bend around wires. MIT, where I got my undergraduate degree, refers to the sensation as "drinking from the fire hose."

Nearly anyone can become turned on to science. The "aha!" moment can arrive in a variety of ways and at any age, and can even jump off the pages of a book or from a moment in a Hollywood movie. If there is a curious child in your life, how do you encourage the spirit without burning down the house? A science career starts with the need to try something purely to see what will happen (sometimes with unexpected, even spectacular, results). One symptom of nascent scientist-hood is a driving need to take everything apart. Trying things with unknown outcomes implies taking occasional strategic risks. In its earliest manifestations, this results in pieces left over when the victimized home appliance is put back together. Risk taking makes sports exciting, and scientists find out early that they thrive on the sensation of trying something intellectually hard – and succeeding. Figuring out a bit of physics isn't as visual as nailing a double somersault in gymnastics class, but the sensation can be the same. Let's look at some memories scientists and engineers have of their first intellectual swan dive (or splashy cannonball!).

Building on Experience

"When I was four or five," says Sir Martin, "I had two baked bean cans and a piece of string, and I played with my sister down the garden." Sir Martin Sweeting is chief executive officer of Surrey Satellite Systems of Guildford, England, an aerospace company that does things like developing spacecraft to manage disaster relief. Of his two cans and string, he says, "This ability to communicate at a distance fascinated me and when I got a little older, about ten years old, we got headsets." Next, it was playing around with building radios. In those days before the internet and cheap long distance, he loved speaking to people around the world freely on his ham radio set. Sweeting was 16 or 17 years old in the Apollo era, and the moon flights launching on the other side of the Atlantic inspired him to "go to university" and eventually obtain a PhD.

Professor Sweeting attributes much of his science and engineering intuition to the government surplus radio and other parts readily available in post-World War II England. He worries that today, "A lot of children lose the concept of real safety and danger. Pick up a soldering iron, burn your finger, and you don't ever do it again. Everything is protected to such an extent that there are real dangers out there [that will be encountered by today's kids] and they'll be out of their depth." He says that human beings learn by their mistakes, and that science teaching needs to recapture that. "Kits of bits isn't enough. The key thing would be to find those really inspirational teachers to get students to do more than they think they could."

Sweeting tells the story of Geoff Perry, a Northern England physics teacher who really excited his elementary school students in the 1960s. He got interested in Sputnik and computed the orbit of early Soviet satellites. His students would make observations of Soviet satellites as they passed overhead, pick up signals, and so on, using just pencil, paper and slide rule.

To excite kids about science, Sweeting says, you "have to expose kids when they are very young – between five and ten, since that's the point at which they are most inquisitive and don't get distracted by the pressures of the world. Somehow, get them to have a practical involvement in that excitement. No matter what field it's in, it's the practicality of it. Not just have it all laid out for them, make it where they have to struggle a bit. I'm not sure that putting it all on the computer is as exciting." Today's electronic technology is so packaged that it's difficult to get inside, he worries, unlike when he could take apart government-surplus radios. "Now it's robots and things like this. Mostly they tend to get their pleasure out of computer games. I feel that it's really important that young people have a practical feeling for how you physically make something. We're losing that so fast."

Sweeting isn't the only one who learned engineering by building seemingly mundane things. "One of the big events for me was my dad retired when I was in sixth grade, and we moved to a farm," says Chris Kitts, head of the Robotics Systems Lab at Santa Clara University in the heart of California's Silicon Valley. "When I was 16 or 17, we built a barn and put it into use. The notion of going through that whole process – I'll never forget that. I remember taking day-by-day photos." In his Central Pennsylvania rural neighborhood, 45 percent of the graduating seniors enlisted in the military. Chris did that, but stopped off at Princeton, where, emboldened by his barn-raising success, he and a buddy built an ultralight aircraft. Princeton became so worried they would kill themselves flying it that they were supervised cutting the craft in half.

These days, Kitts runs a university lab in which undergraduate and graduate students work together to make robots. Among other things, these creations explore the bottom of Lake Tahoe and are launched into space. He says of the ability of his students to try out really building robots, "Hands-on experience lets them go through hypothesis testing. They go off on their own tangents. The next step is matching it up with the real engineering analysis. The practical tinkering stuff you can do better if you inform it with engineering analysis."

I always wonder: If I had grown up in the computer-chip age and not in the era of vacuum-tube TVs, would I have learned as much about how things are put together? Today when I analyze a problem in my head or on paper, I still find myself hanging the problem on mental scaffolding that looks a lot like the guts of a 1960s TV. Sweeting has it right: The only way to learn to build the frames of great ideas in your head is to take apart a lot of things and see how far you get putting them back together.

The Equation

Ilearned how things worked at an electrician's knee, so it's not too surprising that my earliest memories involve the practical. Engineers and scientists, though, go beyond the electrician's *how* to fix physical things to understanding the theory about *why* things work the way they do. Often, rules about why things are the way they are can be captured in *equations* – abstract mathematical relationships. Equations are sometimes based on observations or from using some mathematics on other equations. In any case, they allow prediction of how the world behaves.

The science experience can start with equations just as easily as it can with soldering irons. Some years ago in New Jersey, a five- or six-year-old boy demanded of his chemical engineer father: "Tell me an equation, Daddy." Obligingly, Daddy presented the gift of the Ideal Gas Equation, discovered about 300 years earlier by Robert Boyle. This equation says that if the temperature of a gas (like air) goes up, so will its pressure. The two pulled out one of the first calculators and figured out how the pressure of the air around them might change as it got colder or hotter.

"My primordial equation," sighs George Musser, now an editor at *Scientific American* magazine. "I get a frisson of excitement thinking about it." But the equation wasn't the end of it. Later excursions as an eight-year-old using a telescope to see Comet Kohoutek solidified a desire to observe and measure things, further encouraged by his third- and fourth-grade teachers. Speaking from his Manhattan editorial office, Musser rewinds his memory to Mr. Edgerton guiding fourth-graders to build a simple calculator from potentiometers – devices that change the turn of a dial into electrical resistances. Seeing the machine they had built actually work was a powerful thing. "I did define myself as a science-oriented person as far back as I can remember," he recalls, reading science books (even during recess!) far back into his past.

Becoming a scientist, he says, is a process of winnowing, not sieving. "Kids start with a remarkably broad series of interests," and the tragedy is that often an adult will turn off an interest inadvertently. He recalls that he had a teacher who wanted to "squash art and music" in her students. He wonders what other interests he might enjoy today if those interests had not been pruned as early as they were.

Cowboys, Spaceships and Baker Street

Not every scientist-to-be starts out with activities that involve getting into a lot of trouble. Not everyone has exposure to someone who fixes televisions or writes equations. For the rest, sometimes the first adventures and role models live on the pages of a book. I certainly tried to read as many books as I could during the summer the New York City Public Library featured its moon program. Every book you read earned a dot that you could put on a map of the moon; I couldn't wait to finish another book so that I could go to another spot on the moon!

A few years before I was staying up late on summer nights to earn my self-adhesive colored dots in New York, second-grader Charlie Mobbs was making his weekly search of the San Antonio, Texas, bookmobile. The bookmobile traveled around to schools, like his, with limited or no libraries. He was hunting for his favorite reading material – books about cowboys or dogs. Sadly, they were all checked out. But what was this – a picture book: *Sun, Moon and Stars.*

"It captured my imagination. I loved that book," says Charles Mobbs, now associate professor of neuroscience and geriatrics at Mt. Sinai Medical School in Manhattan. "Then I discovered the shelf in the bookmobile called Science Fiction." Soon, Robert Heinlein was keeping him company at home, followed quickly by just about every other science fiction writer. After that, his undergraduate future at MIT and graduate work at USC were foregone conclusions. "To know what you want to do your whole life is a great gift," he says softly, just the smallest Texas twang left from the streets of San Antonio.

Mobbs isn't the only one to enter the profession through the printed page. Chris Rapley, director of the British Antarctic Survey, these days works the puzzles involved in maintaining Britain's scientific presence at the bottom of the world. Rapley is in charge of about 420 people, bases with names like Halley V (named after the Astronomer Royal who discovered Halley's comet – they keep renumbering it as the ice melts and they have to relocate farther inland), and the ships RSS *Ernest Shackleton* and *James Clark Ross*. Thus, he could hardly be unaware of Britain's scientific history and heritage.

However, Rapley was drawn into science from another bit of British tradition altogether. "The irony is that my English teacher at the age of 11 got me into science by giving me Sherlock Holmes," he laughs. He says that Holmes was a "horizontal thinker," teaching him to carefully gather evidence to spell out what had actually happened, deduced from a whole range of clues. The best part, of course, was when Holmes figured out the case, beginning to end. "That kind of eureka! moment – when I started doing science I discovered that was exactly what science was about," he enthuses now, "when suddenly everything falls into place, whether through a bit of math or modeling."

Asked whether Holmes was his only inspiration, he notes that he was blessed with good teachers. To make the point that any given inspiration might lead various places, he says, "I actually had a good chemistry teacher and that's why I did physics." In any case, he lives now in the spotlight that polar science occupies as the ice at the poles shows signs of dramatic melting, with implications for shorelines everywhere. How does he handle the complex, interdisciplinary, controversial work? His explanation could have been worked out at 221B Baker Street: "The real world, not the world that you might imagine, is all about finding the truth."

The Spark

L ike my own soldering iron adventures, many scientists perform an early experiment involving a closer-up view of hazardous household items than one or both parents would prefer. Microbiologist Barry Chess, now associate professor of natural sciences at Pasadena City College, shakes his head and smiles at the image he has of a metal fork in his five-year-old hand. What would happen, he had wondered, if he pushed it *just so* into a particular electrical socket? The spectacular results of this science experiment – involving a suddenly blacked-out California home – still spread a wide grin across his face. He is amazed by how little trouble he got into at the time. "Very shortly thereafter, I found myself in a class about how things work for pre-kindergartners."

This risk-taking might make parents of young talent bite their nails a bit, like the parents of a gymnast who might look away during certain moves. Also, like parents of young athletes, they need to find a good coach so that Junior learns without injury. "I was always cutting things open," remembers Chess, who now encourages his own students to take things apart. He describes his job teaching community college biology as "trying to teach people to think." As a faculty member training students who will go on to be medical technicians, dental assistants or radiologists, Chess works to help the students in his lab classes understand the need to be careful observers. "The only thing you can measure is how different something is from a control. For example, how do you know you're sick?" He urges his students to find ways of making the subjective measurable. "You can take your temperature," for example, rather than depend on vague feelings of the blahs. He says that too many people just can't "connect the dots" between cause and effect – and, worse, might not even be trying very hard to figure out why it's important to connect them.

Chess is acutely aware of how crucial a faculty mentor can be. He began grad school under the mentorship of a well-known biologist. Partway through his PhD, Chess returned home from a long overseas trip and opened a newspaper to discover that his advisor had committed suicide. Science is a game in which every individual is precious and has a unique contribution; Chess' advisor was really the only one working in his field. Since the department had no one else who really could guide him in his work, this ended his formal education. That was a long time ago. Now, in the midst of cheery chaos, glassware and books, he tries to generate a spark in his own students – or, at least, to make them think. Curiosity can be encouraged but is impossible to teach!

Teachers and parents are not the only science coaches. Michele Glidden has a degree in English and a background in journalism, and says she never did a science fair project (or dissected anything!) herself. However, as the person responsible for managing one of the most prestigious science fairs in the world, she holds a lot of career hopes and dreams in her hands. Glidden is director of science education programs at Science Service, which runs the Intel Science Talent Search (formerly the Westinghouse Science Talent Search) with five- and six-figure scholarships at stake. The fair was in its 57th year in 2006, and, says Glidden, "We have an affiliated fair network that has grown over the years" to cover 46 states. Says Glidden, "The science community has gotten the idea of being a mentor." Many students who enter the Intel Talent Search work in a scientist's lab, allowing them to achieve real results beyond the unguided tinkering that otherwise might occur. Some students do projects in their garages, and some students simply cannot get access to a lab. Despite the resources at any given student's disposal, she says, "There will always be Olympic athletes," and there will always be great scientists that come up out of the ranks. How do we encourage them and find them, or would they all have found themselves? Sometimes it takes someone who just decides to go out beating the bushes, like Gil Moore.

Gil Moore was born in 1928 and, when asked how he got into science, says that he mostly remembers trying to stay alive in the post-Depression economy of the time. He did, however, arrive at New Mexico State University in 1945, just as the German V2 rockets captured at the end of World War II began to be analyzed and flown at nearby White Sands Missile Range. "The real fire in my belly came from watching those vapor trails over the Organ Mountains," he remembers. In 1946, the Army brought over a V2 and put it in a parade; Moore has a picture of himself next to it. In 1947, he was offered "grunt work" at White Sands at the then-princely salary of 65 cents an hour (a huge raise from his 35-cent-an-hour job in a chemistry lab!) Moore went on to a career that spanned the entire space program; after his first attempt at retirement in 1987, his wife asked him, "What do you want to do when you grow up?" He decided to travel the country and try to do what he could to excite kids about science.

He started taking a rocket into classrooms. He fired it at the start of class and told the students that if they did not go to sleep or talk among themselves, he would fire it again at the end of class. Attention was rapt. He developed a list of home phone numbers of physics teachers; he called them at home and asked if he could come speak to their classes. No one ever said no, and typically he gave about six lectures a day.

Moore says, "Once I was in Idaho Falls and lectured at a third-grade class and then lectured to a junior high class and then to a high school class." All were from the same economic stratum. With the third-grade kids, "you'd start to talk and *zing* – up the hands would go." Pretty dang smart questions would be asked, he says, and kids would be bubbling over with ideas. Then he got to the junior high class and got a lot of questions – more intelligent and better-grounded ones than from the smaller kids. When he got to the high school, three students were asleep in the front row, and there were practically no questions. Based on that, he decided to come up with a project to capture kids' imaginations at the key age of junior high.

To apply Moore's philosophy of "hands-on, brains-on science," students created parts of an actual spacecraft, named Starshine. This spacecraft allowed students to measure how far Earth's atmosphere was extending into space on any given day. The atmosphere expands and contracts a bit depending on a variety of things. If it were bigger and puffier than usual, then spacecraft around the Earth would go overhead at a different time than if the atmosphere were smaller. When a lot of students measured the time that Starshine went overhead for a few months, their data could be put together to get an overall picture. To make it easy to see from the ground, Starshine resembled a high-tech disco ball: a sphere covered with small mirrors. Students were sent kits to grind and polish these mirrors. For the first one, Moore's house became a kit factory. His wife, Phyllis, built most of the kits, 12 or 15 hours a day, seven days a week, for about four months, periodically hauling a huge bag to the post office. Gradually they got some help, first from Jackson State University in Alabama and then from various schools and corporations, and Starshine has remained an all-volunteer project.

"We've had such wonderful messages from teachers," Moore says. Teachers say: "This is the first time that our kids have been interested in anything to do with math and science." Project Starshine sent three unpolished mirrors to a class in a given school. Each mirror occupied about ten kids, who competed with each other to do the best job. It takes a couple hours or so to grind a mirror by hand; students would get tired, and pass it around. "Grind and grind and grind, polish and polish and polish," as Moore cheerfully describes the process, with excitement building once the students could begin to see themselves reflected. They'd send Moore the best two mirrors and keep one for the school trophy case. The very best would be attached to the spacecraft and go to space. Various engineering organizations donated services for final preparation of the mirrors and assembly of the spacecraft.

Three Starshines have been flown (one launched in 1999, two in 2001) and all generated excellent data on the atmosphere. As of late 2006, a paired fourth and fifth craft (built by students in 43 nations) are mothballed waiting for a ride to space. Eventually all Starshine spacecraft fall into the Earth's atmosphere and burn up; Starshine 3 reentered January 21, 2003, and so there has been a gap in the program since. Moore says, "You can't turn science on and off," and waits, frustrated, for student spacecraft launch to become a national priority again. Meanwhile, Moore (who is fond of pointing out that he has 60 years of experience in aerospace) has become a passionate advocate for his brand of hands-on, brains-on science, in which a young student can say, "Hey. I did that, that's mine." He emphasizes: Let students get involved in science, and don't have students simply be observers of a professional science elite. If you do, there might be no elite left 20 years hence!

Coming Back Around

Recently my Dad, now in his nineties, decided to entrust me with his electrician's toolbox. The treasure chest included some beautiful old instruments, with knobs and dials that I remember from my earliest soldering days (but was not allowed to touch back then!) They're probably less accurate than their modern digital equivalents, but they still work – and when I look at them I can hear him say, "That's your problem, *right there.*" They remind me that scientists learn by trying things out for themselves. If you're reading this book, you're interested in seeing how scientists work. Well, let's get to it: Now that I have my Dad's toolbox, I can get out in front of you with authority and tell you where the problems are, right *here* and *here* and *here*!

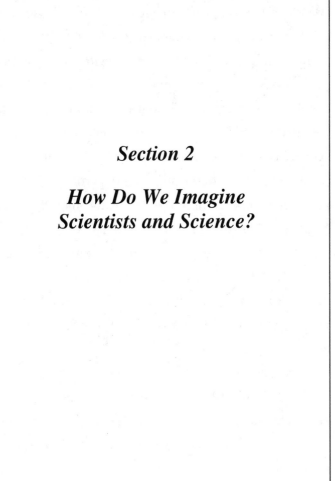

Section 2

*How Do We Imagine
Scientists and Science?*

Typical Scientist

If I were to say, "He is a typical scientist," that would trigger a certain image in your mind. How do we develop the image of a "typical scientist?" (Or, for that matter, a typical *anything*?) Whether we admit it or not, we all operate with stereotypes of professions, often enhanced and reinforced by images in television and film. As someone who is female, five foot two and blonde, I have the advantage that everyone remembers me since normally I'm one of the few people fitting that description in my particular specialty, aerospace engineering. (Not looking like a "typical engineer" has the disadvantage that while everyone might know *my* name I still have to squint up at name badges!). I usually wear a bright-colored jacket, too, and then I know that being the "short lady in the yellow jacket" will let people find me in a crowded room at an engineering or science meeting.

You may have noticed that I talk about both scientists and engineers in this book, and to this point have not made much distinction between the two. I'm a bit of each, which would make me an *applied scientist* to some people and a *research and development engineer* to others. My particular case aside, though, scientists discover new knowledge that engineers then apply to solve real-world problems. There are more similarities than differences for the purposes of this book; we will explore the distinction between scientists and engineers in depth in Section 4. Accepting that I'm not the stereotype of the "typical rocket scientist," who is? Is he good or evil? Brilliant? Even just lumping together all "scientists" loses the distinction between a laboratory chemist and a theoretical physicist, or even the broad array of jobs encompassed by science, engineering and mathematics. In the popular imagination, all typical scientists are male, frumpy dressers and wearers of horn-rimmed glasses with tape on the nosepiece.

When I'm not in my la-BOR-atory engineering spacecraft, I work with various groups to encourage screenwriters to develop scientist characters that are not one-note stereotypes. I say: Lose the bubbling test tubes, the diabolical laughter and the lab coats. This is difficult for writers because the stereotype is an easy storytelling device – shorthand that requires little or no explanation. If we see someone with test tubes in a basement, we know he is up to no good, right? I challenge writers anyway: Why are there no sitcoms about a science lab? Why is there no TV next-door neighbor who just happens to be a scientist, as opposed to a lawyer, a doctor or an auto mechanic? The reasons: "It takes too much explanation." "It will slow the story down." "No one will understand it." "Too much action takes place in their heads." Of course, most of these objections would apply equally well to a lawyer, who spends a lot of time preparing before entering the drama of a courtroom. Writers have no trouble focusing on the exciting part of the law without delving too much into the detailed process.

The process of discovering the truth and its impacts is inherently good theater. For example, the film *Erin Brockovich* is based on a true story of a legal assistant who tried to find out whether water in a small town was being contaminated by a large utility. The film generated a lot of interest in testing water for the chromium-6 pollutant portrayed in the movie. The dramatic tension in the film comes from Erin's character (played by Julia Roberts) gradually extracting information and pulling together a big picture from many pieces. Science's methods and those of detective work are similar, as is the excitement generated when an answer comes into focus. The various crime lab TV shows have popularized the process of investigation, as evidenced by a large increase in college criminology majors since its debut.

Is all exposure good exposure, or is it better to skip a story that might give the wrong message? Once I needed to find science consultants for a student film about the perceived evils of cloning. For help, I called a professor whose research interests were in plant genetics. Plant cloning has been around for centuries, but somehow recent advances have been extrapolated to Frankenstein with nothing in between: A case of a sea of hype threatening to drown some nice, close-in and practical applications. At any rate, the professor required a few of his biology graduate students to stick around one Friday to show the lab to the film graduate students. With clear trepidation on both sides, the two groups of graduate students hung out together for an afternoon. The film students discovered to their disappointment how routine and harmless the work was (and how closely a key piece of equipment resembled a toaster). The film was not made and everyone went on to other things. Is this a good outcome? On the one hand, it avoided adding to the pile of "evil scientist" imagery out there. Still, another story about science was not written and an opportunity for a positive story was missed.

Science Fiction

W hen we try to think of a scientist character in a movie, most often the ones that come to mind first are from the realm of science fiction. In the 1950s, science fiction was often about "what if we could go into space?" As spaceflight has become more routine, what-ifs have migrated into the realms of biology and genetic engineering. Say "science fiction," though, and a spacecraft often is still the first thing to come to mind. The *Star Wars* franchise has grossed billions of dollars based on morality plays set on alien planets; the evergreen *Star Trek* series have all done well for their creators. But the excitement (and even cultism) associated with some of these films doesn't extend to fandom for real science. Why is that?

John Copeland has spent a lifetime in television and film as producer of science fiction, westerns, and documentaries about a wide range of topics. Copeland strives for accurate science in his productions, a trait that has earned him legions of fans among the scientifically trained. I asked him: Why do people go to space movies but do not clamor for increases in NASA's budget? He worries that scientific institutions have not learned to convey the "exotic excitement" of discovery. "Part of being able to concisely communicate an idea [to the public] and instill your enthusiasm is that you have to be able to communicate on their level. And, many scientists are incapable of doing that. They are so steeped in technical jargon of academia, the papers they write, that they presuppose the person they are talking to already has knowledge." He does, however, know scientists who do communicate well – particularly those who teach introductory courses or deal with the public regularly.

Copeland says that a spokesperson who can really relate science is crucial. For example, he says, global warming issues are complex and polarizing. The big problem for everyday people is: What does it mean to me? What can I do? Why should I care? Copeland quoted a Greek proverb: "A culture which is truly great is where old men plant trees knowing they will never sit in their shade." The trick, though, is that somehow scientific institutions have to give the public enough information about where to plant those trees as the world changes faster and faster. To make it even more difficult, he adds, "a lot of folks have a stereotypical view of a scientist – maybe a bit threatening."

How should a scientist (or the field they study) be portrayed in a movie or a TV series? For Copeland, "When we present something in a dramatized form we present stuff for the audience in absolutes. It will either be this or that." Scientists, though, are often uncomfortable giving a black-or-white answer (since more knowledge is always being discovered) and will take pains to say that they are still studying something. Understanding that science is an ongoing evolution is hard for people to wrap their heads around, since we all like neat and tidy answers. Answers are rarely wrapped up and tied with a bow in real life, and consequently scientists are burdened with telling people that the truth is something they might not want to hear – and also that it might not be easy to explain. Taking all that and making it compelling fiction creates additional challenges.

Many times people first encounter a science idea through a science fiction story. Science fiction is often divided into "hard science fiction" and "fantasy." Hard science fiction is loosely defined as fiction based on science as we understand it now. Sometimes a story might propose that in the future we learn how to do something currently seen as impossible (such as the ability to travel to other stars faster than the speed of light) with some sort of explanation about how that might happen. Fantasy stories, on the other hand, occur in another universe (with dragons, magic and so on) and there is usually no attempt to be scientifically accurate (although many "worlds," like those of *Harry Potter*, try to at least be internally consistent).

Greg Bear is a writer who is usually characterized as working in the area of hard science fiction, lately publishing several works in the realm of where biology might lead us in the near future. He says, "A billion years from now will they say we had it all right? So how wrong are we? We have to think outside the box to figure out how we can be right, which is the point of science fiction." There is a bit of scientist in every science fiction writer, he says. Bear says that all science fiction is the dreams that scientists have when they're trying to figure out great problems – they have to imagine what's going to happen next if things go on the way they are going. He says, "Science is taking yourself and your desires out of the equation when you look at something."

Scientists also think about how things might possibly work, and then develop ways to test whether or not they are right. (This process will be described in Section 3.) The big difference between writing fiction and doing science is that the scientists are obliged to prove themselves right (or not) whereas an author just needs to get you to suspend disbelief. However, thinking up the questions to ask ("What if we could use bacteria as tiny factories to make cheap antimalaria drugs for the third world?") is just as creative an endeavor whether it is intended to drive a story or a research program. And, despite stereotypes to the contrary, most scientists spend a lot of time thinking about how their work might be used in society, as we will discuss in Section 5 of this book.

As an engineer, I like to read science fiction (particularly hard science fiction) because I can learn something in an entertaining way. Often when I read a story, I will end up searching the internet to see whether the author's premise indeed reflects current science (or is made up of whole cloth). Although I can't think of any instance where I directly solved an engineering problem because of an analogous fictional solution, the energy I put into solving problems in a science fiction story along with the characters is certainly good practice! As we discussed in Section 1, science is in many ways like a sport, in terms of discipline and the need to get in there and try things yourself to really learn. For me, reading science fiction and trying to keep up with the characters is like a good pick-up game for a basketball player – keeps me in practice and lets me know the talent on the street!

Sometimes the links are more direct. Science fiction writer Arthur C. Clarke invented the idea of a geosynchronous communication satellite and first published a description in 1945, long before the first SYNCOM satellite in 1963. A geosynchronous satellite is one that is in an orbit so high above the Earth's equator (22,300 miles, or 35,800 km) that it takes 24 hours to orbit once. (For reference, the Space Shuttle's typical orbit, usually a bit more than 200 miles [320 km] above the surface of the Earth, takes about 90 minutes.) Since the ground underneath also takes 24 hours to rotate (the Earth turns once a day), that means that a geosynchronous satellite appears to stay over a certain spot on Earth. This is very convenient for broadcasting to a particular geographic region. Today, certain "slots" in geosynchronous orbit over heavily populated areas are so popular that parking satellites there has to be adjudicated by the Geneva-based International Telecommunication Union (ITU) – a part of the future that even Clarke did not foresee. True, Clarke was both an engineer and a science fiction writer, with a background in radio and physics – but he went beyond predicting a piece of hardware and predicted a future of communications flashed around the world.

Aliens, Comets and Portents

S ometimes the public gets a little fuzzy on what scientific capabilities we actually have now, versus those that exist only in science fiction television. When I worked at the Jet Propulsion Laboratory (JPL), the NASA center that runs planetary exploration, and gave public talks, more often than you might think someone would ask me why we were wasting money sending probes to planets using rockets. After all, everyone has seen instantaneous ways to send probes (and people) to their otherworldly destinations on their favorite TV shows. I never did find a good way to politely explain the difference between fantasy and reality, and usually asked why, if the technology existed, airlines didn't offer that means of transport from Los Angeles to Denver. This would generally trigger comments about "the government" keeping the technology secret (except, presumably, from science fiction writers). Government cover-ups of key technologies is an unfortunate theme that makes for good storytelling, but can frustrate scientists whose discoveries fall into areas the public wants to believe "the government" is working on and keeping from them. Notable among these areas is visits by aliens to Earth.

Along those lines, what happens if a scientist makes a discovery, and amateurs decide to "help" with observations down the line? Suppose further that reporters covering the story do not quite make clear what is actually observed by professionals versus speculation with roots in the wishful thinking of science-fiction fans? Astronomer Alan Hale found himself hoeing just that row. Hale runs the nonprofit Earthrise Institute near the rural village of Cloudcroft, New Mexico. On the night of July 23, 1995, Hale was out observing known comets. Comet hunting was something of a hobby for him, although he is a professional astronomer. To find a new comet, says Hale, you sweep a telescope back and forth "looking for things that shouldn't be there" according to existing star charts – particularly for fuzzy things, rather than the bright points of stars. Other indistinct objects, such as diffuse nebulae in the telescope's field of view, complicate the search for undiscovered comets.

Astronomers get to know the sky and, after a while, can identify objects that should be there. On that night, though, Hale realized that he had seen something not yet recorded on star charts, and emailed his finding to the Central Bureau for Astronomical Telegrams, which keeps tracks of such things. The next morning he found out that he had indeed found a new comet, and that Tom Bopp, an amateur astronomer in Arizona, had also found it that same night. The comet became, by convention, Hale-Bopp, or (officially) C/1995 O1. By

1997, it became visible to the unaided eye as a bright comet with a double tail.

A photographer who did not have a good knowledge of the sky and of how to take astronomical pictures mistook a faint star near the comet for a "Saturn-like object" trailing the comet as it approached Earth. In the subsequent press coverage, this mutated into an alien spacecraft following the comet. When Hale explained the reality and the mistake that had been made, he was called an "Earth traitor" and worse for "withholding information." He told people to go out and look at the comet themselves, but people apparently either would believe what they wanted without looking for themselves, or would convince themselves that some nearby star or another was the "spaceship."

This would have simply been irritating to Hale and died out in due course, but instead took a tragic and bizarre turn. Comets have been seen since antiquity as portents, and somehow old superstitions have managed to hang on into the age of modern communications and in some ways to be amplified by it. Cult leader Marshall Applewhite apparently convinced his followers in San Diego to commit mass suicide so that they could go to heaven on the "spaceship" following Hale-Bopp. The 39 bodies of Applewhite's Heaven's Gate cultists were found on March 26, 1997. They were all dressed alike and wearing armbands proclaiming them the "Heaven's

Gate Away Team," a presumed reference to teams that left their spaceships to explore new worlds in classic science fiction stories. To attempt to separate fact from fiction, Hale called a press conference in Cloudcroft (then population 622), which drew media from all over the country.

The more dubious information builds up, the harder it is for the average person to focus on the things that have actually been observed. Worse, the line between science fact and science fiction fuzzes up – with, as we have seen here, sometimes tragic results. This drives scientists nuts. "Science is not a democracy," says Hale. "It's based on preponderance of evidence." When reporters try to "balance" a story (or make it "more newsworthy") they may quote people who hold views outside the scientific mainstream. This means a story may run quoting someone without qualifications and with easily disproved hypotheses (like a star being mistaken for a spaceship coming to save the believers). Although this case was extreme, it was the result of an accumulation of news reports and other information: some accurate and balanced, some sensationalized, some word of mouth. This is what scientists fear when their work "makes news" – that they will go from a regime in which they pursue truth through years of careful accumulation of evidence, to one in which communication is instant and deadlines are short.

Journalists have to compile information and push it out in a matter of hours. No wonder confusion can ensue when these two worlds intersect!

Science Reality Meets Science Fiction

Donna Shirley is uniquely qualified to discuss how science fiction and science fact feed each other. She spent many years at JPL, where her last engagement before she retired was directing the Mars Exploration Program. Later, though, she was the founding director of the Science Fiction Museum and Hall of Fame in Seattle. I asked her: What are some trends in science fiction, and do they in some way predict trends in real science?

Shirley offers the opinion that people are decreasing in their interest in hard science fiction and increasing in their appetite for fantasy. "When I was a kid," she says, "escapism *was* science fiction." The problem is that spacecraft are now science fact, and to compensate, space-oriented science fiction has outstripped reality so far that they've become fantasy. "The thing is," Shirley says, "you get back to swords and sorcery." Fiction can still fire the imagination, whereas many aspects of real science are just not presented in a way that excites people and draws them into the detective story of science.

The fast pace of science itself creates challenges for writers. Shirley notes that as science gains more knowledge of alien places (like the surface of Mars), the people who write science fiction have to be scientists or engineers themselves, or at least consult with them.

Edgar Rice Burroughs could write Martian fantasies in the 1910s and '20s because no one knew what the surface of Mars looked like. Now, if a writer is going to write about Mars he's got to take off from the current groundwork. Compared to the research required to write about a trip to Mars, Shirley notes that it's a lot easier to postulate a universe with dragons that fly and talk, at least in terms of needing to interview scientists for background.

Why does fiction sell better than fact? Some of it is storytelling – if a work of fiction has clearly identified Good Guys and Bad Guys, we can identify with the characters without much effort. No background research is required before reading the novel. However, if a storyteller elects to pick and chose what information to present (or to misquote a source), without background, you'll never know. Scientists themselves feel excitement in the discovery inherent in their work, but it's an excitement that is hard to convey effectively to the armchair observer. Without actually studying a field yourself, it's harder to feel the "aha" moment when all the pieces fall together, unless an expert has laid out all those pieces for you. A reader has to work harder, to learn about something relatively abstract, which includes full discussion of many uncertainties instead of asserting one right answer. I often have people pointing out cool "new" discoveries to me – often, things I've read about in science journals (or even textbooks) years before. But I never discourage them, particularly if they seem excited about learning something new!

In the other direction, sometimes real exploration suffers by comparison to science fiction. The public is so used to seeing gee-whiz footage of space battles that real footage of Mars or space launches seems ho-hum. Even if people intellectually know that science fiction is not real, human nature does sometimes invite the comparison between real and imagined spacecraft. On the other hand science fiction that shows a far future world with evil applications of a particular technology might block an important piece of real-life research. Readers might assume that one early step necessarily leads down the pictured dark path – even if everyone acknowledges that the path is fictional!

The great irony of the limited choices in "true science" entertainment is that science is a giant detective story, inherently richer in twists and turns than any invented world could be. How are the mysteries solved, and how does one area of science build on the next? What are the nonstereotypical scientists like anyway? The next two sections will let you try the discovery process out for yourself, and then meet some different types of scientists, without a pair of taped-up glasses in sight.

Section 3

How Do Scientists Think?

The Scientific Method

You have lost your keys again. You *just had* them, and you needed to be out the door five minutes ago. The first thing you do is try to remember where you saw them last. In the door? So, you go to the door and then to the kitchen counter. Pockets in the last coat you remember wearing? No luck anywhere. No one is home but you; they have to be somewhere. Finally, you retrace your steps all the way out to the garage and find them sitting right where you left them: up on the roof of the car. You must have put them there when you got the last package from the back seat! If you are short, you might never have found them until someone taller came into the garage and asked what your keys were doing on the car roof.

A scientist is someone who looks at the facts and behavior of the world in an orderly way, then uses that knowledge to solve a problem or to predict something. (There are niceties here about what part of this is science versus engineering, but more on that later!) In the example above, with your keys, you are taking a scientific approach. You have a list in your head of the places you normally put your keys. You also have a set of assumptions and knowledge about the world that you rarely have to spell out for yourself or anyone else – until a problem arises. Then you slow down and start to recite your assumptions and habits: "I know I opened the door, so I had them then. I put down the groceries, and I had on the green coat." You decided to check those places, and, when there was no success, concluded that because keys do not move on their own, if you were to revisit all the places you had been since you last saw your keys, you would find them.

Scientists call this process the *scientific method.* First, you collect *data.* Here the data would be all the times you've observed yourself, without thinking about it, putting your keys somewhere when you come into the house. Next, you develop a *hypothesis* – a best prediction given the data you have (my keys are missing but are probably in the door). Finally, you *test* the hypothesis (by looking at the door) and reject it (since the keys aren't there) and continue to develop new hypotheses until such time as the facts fit the new hypothesis (you find your keys). Once a hypothesis proves to a reasonable degree to fit the way the world works, it becomes a *theory.*

We could develop any hypothesis we wanted to about where our keys have gotten to. Testing our hypothesis, though, and elevating it to a theory, requires observing how the world actually works. For example, you presumably have never dug a hole in the yard, dropped your keys in and covered them up. Thus, there is no need to look in the yard (but there might be, if you share your space with intrepid small children who just discovered the concept of buried treasure). Most of us stick to a tightly controlled, rational approach when we need an answer quickly, but rarely analyze this process of developing a theory.

So, if we are all scientists, why does science seem so alien to most of us? Part of it is because scientists need to know about a lot of specialized stuff. In other words, to make progress scientists have to learn what others have discovered already about how certain parts of the world work. If you don't know about existing antibiotics and our best theories about how they kill bacteria, it's hard to figure out how to search for a new one. If you don't know the physics of how an airplane works, you have to recreate more than a hundred years of experiments on your own. Another alien thing is the language. Often scientists invent new words for things to simplify the way they talk to others in their field. We all do it every day; ten years ago, describing an iPod (or, for that matter, the internet) would have taken a paragraph or more. But you know what one is and probably either own one or have a kid who does; you use the shorthand *iPod* for the whole economic system of music you can buy and store to play any time you want. Think about how many things you complain about every day (pop-up ads, slow dial-up) that would have been mumbo-jumbo to you a few years ago.

Scientists have this problem in spades. Their fields change rapidly, and so most fields develop a whole language to describe ideas and help organize facts to make them easier to remember and understand. The trouble, too, is that if instead of calling an iPod an iPod, you called it, "One of those little things made by Apple, Inc., that holds music you download off the internet," you would be terminally uncool. Scientists, being people, also do not like looking uncool to their peers. Therefore, they learn to use their field's jargon, and it's hard for them to turn it off when they talk to nonscientists. Imagine how it would be for you if someone from 1945 landed in your living room and you had to explain all the electronics in your house to him or her. It would be frustrating not to use any of the normal names for things, wouldn't it?

More fundamentally, though, in daily life we cannot question our assumptions as much as a scientist must. For instance, we get up in the morning, walk across the room presuming that gravity will keep us on the floor, and so on. Most of us do not spend our days in games of "what if" but pretty much believe what we see. We don't ask: What if gravity stopped working for five minutes? What would happen? What new things could I learn while the gravity was off? We believe what we see and for many purposes this serves us well.

We See Only What We Believe

Often, we see only what we believe – a trait that scientists have to work to suppress. Try the following experiment: Cut yourself a strip of ordinary paper, say 11 inches long by about two inches wide. Put a half-twist in it and tape the two ends together as shown in the illustration. You will now have a weird-looking ring known as a Mobius strip.

Now, paper has two sides to it, right? Try drawing a line down the center of your strip. It meets up! You have created a piece of paper that has only one side! Is that possible? How can paper only have one side? But there it is – you have one in your hands. Try coloring one edge. What happens?

Now try cutting it in thirds ... what happens? Is *that* possible? A scientist would find this exciting and would play with it for a while. Are you a scientist?

This experience (presuming you have not seen a Mobius strip before) is similar to what happens when scientists see a piece of data that does not fit any existing theory. How can they broaden their theory to take in this new data? Do they have to come up with a new theory? Did you like the feeling of discovering what a Mobius strip could do, or did it make you vaguely uneasy? By the way, this phenomenon was discovered in 1848 by August Mobius, a German mathematician, and at nearly the same time by Johann Benedict Listing. It led to a burst of new mathematics that continues to be important to theoretical physics today.

Different Ways of "Doing Science"

Scientists can be split into three very broad types: observers, experimentalists and theoreticians. In practice, most are a bit of each. As the names would imply, observers look at the world around them without trying to change anything. Experimenters try to change something about the world in a controlled way to see what happens. Theoreticians, on the other hand, look at the data collected by observers and experimenters, and (usually using math and computers) try to decide what is going on and to predict what will happen in the future (if a particular experiment were to be performed, for instance). In our example about finding your keys, you were a theoretician when you stopped to think about where your keys might be and why. Then you defined some observations and experiments that needed to be done to find them!

All types of scientists have to be careful observers of the world and be very conscious of their assumptions so that if they make a mistake they don't assume right away that they've discovered something new. (Well, OK, they might get excited for a while, but then they calm down and start paying attention again.) It can be pretty embarrassing if a scientist announces a "new discovery" to the world, only to find out it was all a mistake. Scientists hate it when that happens.

How do scientists check that they have not made mistakes? They first double check how they made each observation – was there anything unusual going on that day? Could anything have affected their measurements? If you buy shoes on a hot day, and your feet tend to swell, you know you should keep that in mind when choosing a size. In the same way, scientists also have to allow for outside effects and check their experimental process, conditions during the experiment and whether they might have missed something.

If you are balancing your checkbook and the amount of money you think you have does not match what the bank says you have, a few things could have gone wrong. You might have added or subtracted wrong, you might have written down the amount of a check wrong or you might have forgotten to write in a check altogether. As you go through figuring out what happened, you might first check your addition and subtraction. If that was not the problem (or if fixing your math made the problem different or worse!), you would go back to the original receipts for the month to see what was going on. So first you would check the process you used to get to your result (your bank balance), and then you would start to check your errors of omission – the things you left out or wrote down wrong. Eventually, you would get everything to balance out.

Scientists do not get a handy statement from the universe each month telling them what their answers should be; instead they check each other – a process called *peer review.* When a scientist is pretty sure that he has a good observation or experiment, he writes a paper about it. Then he sends that paper out to a scientific journal. The editor of that journal then has other scientists review it (often anonymously). These reviewers look carefully both at how the experiment or observation was done (like checking addition in our checkbook example) and also consider whether the authors forgot anything. Then, if the conclusion about how the world works is different than people thought it was before, the reviewers think hard about what else may have gone wrong.

Reviewers will make suggestions to the editor (including, sometimes, having the author re-do the experiment, analyze data in alternative ways, or do other additional work). If everyone agrees that the experiment was done correctly and it does seem that something new was discovered, the paper is published in a science journal. This process is not perfect and, people being people, sometimes an innovative idea does not make it into print or a bad one does. By and large, it serves science well as a way of questioning assumptions and getting more than one pair of eyes on a particular problem.

This continuous questioning also leads to a culture that, broadly speaking, tends to encourage some degree of nonconformity and doubts about authority. If you visit any science department at a major university, it is highly unlikely you will see a suit or tie. This is true, of course, for laboratory scientists who wear lab coats (or more esoteric protective gear). However, many scientists just use a computer, whiteboard and paper all day long and so have a tendency toward jeans and sweatshirts. More significantly, if you try to tell scientists what to do, most of the time they will decide whether you're right, and, if not, will ignore you. Scientists expect this from each other, and when someone with different norms and expectations attempts to collaborate with them, oftentimes misunderstandings occur. But, perhaps scientists are not so different from the rest of us. What would your response have been if early in your search for your keys your spouse had asked, "Looked on the top of the car, Honey?"

Observing Things

In many ways, the oldest activity in science is observing how the world works and then developing a story about why it works that way. Yet scientists, like the short person who could not have seen the keys on the car roof, sometimes cannot solve a problem with existing instruments in their own fields. They have to wait until they figure out how to invent a new instrument, or until someone in a different field happens to turn something built for a different purpose on their problem. (Or they wait until a new hypothesis is put forth that explains a set of observations that did not make sense before.) This is why scientists want to know a lot about how precise a measurement a particular instrument makes. If we want to see how many fleas are on a dog, a picture of a dog a mile away showing the whole dog as a dot is not very useful. It's true that we counted zero fleas on the dog in the picture; it's also meaningless to say so!

Some scientists have to deal with observing things that happened a long time in the past, or reconcile observations taken with instruments of varying quality, such as rainfall measurements taken in 1600 with ones made today. Climate change researchers need the longest possible record of weather to find out how much warmer the world is now than in the distant past.

However, thermometers have only been around for 400 years or so, and good ones for far less time than that. Some people have it even worse. Astronomers must always view their quarry at unthinkable distances and come up with ways to predict behavior that might take millions or billions of years to occur. How do they make progress in the face of such literally astronomical odds?

Astronomer Stephen Unwin guides engineers developing telescopes that will fly in space to look for planets around other stars. New discoveries these days usually require large and complex telescopes to see the subtle effects, for example, of a small planet orbiting a big, distant star. Astronomers as a community have to argue and compete to figure out what equipment should be built, what astronomy is best done in space, what is best done on the ground and so on. Since very few new telescopes are built each year, either on earth or in space, scientists have to know what kinds of experiments they want to do long before anyone starts polishing mirrors. It's like deciding what kind of new car your family will buy: Some people might want a two-seater to zip around in, but you might need to haul things and so you get a truck instead.

No matter what sorts of telescopes are ultimately built, astronomers cannot alter the sky – they can only observe it. Or as Unwin puts it, "I have to take what the sky gives me." Astronomy is largely an observational science. This means that astronomers cannot change anything in the sky and see what happens to validate their theories about how the universe works. What they have to do instead is to figure out ways to make the effect they are looking for at any given time stand out clearly.

Once they have all that figured out, astronomers still have to do a lot of thinking to interpret what they are seeing and to pick the right things to look at in the first place. For example, says Unwin, if you were looking at stars at all different distances and trying to figure out how bright they were, the distance would distort this measurement because closer stars (like one flashlight closer to you than another) would appear brighter. Instead, you would use your knowledge of the sky to find a "cluster" of stars that are all more or less the same distance from the Earth. Then you can look at all the stars and see whether there are more dim ones than bright ones among stars all at the same distance. "You learn how to read them," he says.

One of the cornerstones of science is the ability to do an experiment more than once and get the same result, a trait scientists call *reproducibility*. If an experiment can be reproduced, it is more likely the outcome was not a freak result due to some weird circumstance or something measured incorrectly, which can happen in science just like anyplace else. Since astronomers cannot start the universe over and make the exact same measurement twice, how can they know their data is reproducible? They make measurements multiple times; of course, if the sky is changing astronomers have to do the best they can with data from other, similar objects in the sky. For that reason, astronomers, perhaps more so than other scientists, can't take any one piece of data by itself but must view all the known data in context. That context itself changes continuously as more data is collected.

This raises the question of what happens if a piece of data is measured incorrectly, due to equipment failure or human error. Does it matter? If there is not a lot of data, Unwin says, "because you can't actively do experiments, it's very hard in astronomy to build a coherent picture based on a single event or single piece of data. So testing of a theory requires collecting more data, which will either verify or contradict that theory." In other words, it's back out to the telescope dome for the observers to see whether they've discovered something new or just made a mistake. A balance has to be made between how an observation appears to not fit into established theory (which might mean a new discovery) versus the chances that the data are just plain wrong. "Bad data is worse than no data" is a truism in astronomy, because bad data can waste your time and raise your hopes of a new theory when you might just have recorded some unfortunately timed interference.

As with every other human achievement, someone had to invent an orderly process of observing and explaining the world. The critical piece of this process is the ability to question existing knowledge and to develop new explanations as inconsistencies are developed. Someone somewhere had to dream up a system of keeping track of which facts could be used to draw which types of conclusions. In that respect, philosophers probably developed the very earliest pieces of the puzzle.

Suppose I say, "If I use an expensive shampoo, my hair will be gorgeous." Does that mean that if my hair looks great, I must have used an expensive shampoo? Actually, no – advertising aside, I might just be lucky and have good hair days all the time. We did not say that the *only* way my hair might look great was to use an expensive shampoo. Keeping track of what one can actually infer from observations underlies a lot of what scientists do. The example here goes by the fancy name of *hypothetical syllogism* – we develop a hypothesis (if I use an expensive shampoo, my hair will be gorgeous), make an observation (my hair looks great) and draw a conclusion (therefore I must have really splashed out on shampoo). However, as we say above, we actually can't draw that conclusion from the hypothesis and facts given. These ways of looking carefully at cause and effect are thought to have first been written down by Aristotle about 2,300 years ago, in ancient Greece. It's very easy to develop all sorts of cause-and-effect relationships if you're a casual observer of nature – but scientists make mistakes if they're not very careful about what has to be the cause of an observed effect, and what might be coincidence.

People have probably been doing experiments of one sort or another since well back into prehistory. Developing experiments that follow what we today understand as the scientific method, however, was first clearly articulated in print in Western society by Francis Bacon in the 1600s, and shortly thereafter by members of the Royal Society of London. Officially founded on Nov. 28, 1660, the Royal Society was developed for "natural philosophers" (forerunners of today's scientists) to get together once a week and witness science experiments. Early members included Christopher Wren, Robert Hooke, Robert Boyle and, later, Isaac Newton. Some credit Boyle's vacuum pump as one of the first modern pieces of experimental equipment, and his discovery of what is now called "Boyle's Law" (the relationship between pressure and temperature of a gas) as one of the first experimental discoveries. For centuries before the founding of the Royal Society, the ideas of ancient philosophers and religious texts were accepted without question, and it was considered heretical to actually observe nature and draw conclusions about causes of natural phenomena. Once it became acceptable to observe and measure the world directly and publish the results, science began to advance at a rapid rate.

Sometimes scientists can't measure what they want to measure directly either because an event happened in the past and was not recorded at the time, or because the thing they really want to know is hard to measure. Imagine that you have a black metal box with a powered light bulb inside. You cannot tell from looking at the box whether the light bulb is on – but if you put your hand on the box, you might well be burned if the light *is* on. However, you have no way of telling whether the light was just turned on (and thus the box is not very warm yet) or whether the light has just been turned off but the box is hot because it was on for an hour. Therefore, the temperature of the black metal box is not a perfect indicator of whether the light is on, but it is a generally accurate indicator.

If you could measure instead whether any current is flowing into the box, then you would know with far more certainty whether the light is on, since there is no appreciable time lag between the current flowing or not and the light turning on or off. Therefore, measuring current would be a better *surrogate measure* of whether the light bulb is on or off than feeling the temperature of the box. Using a surrogate measure means that you have to thoroughly understand the process that ties the surrogate to what you want to measure, or you might wind up with misleading data! Coming up with good surrogates is critical in many fields, and one of the key creative skills of a scientist.

Clinical medicine uses surrogate measurements all the time. An electrocardiogram (ECG) measures different electrical voltages on your skin, then creates a squiggly line that is interpreted to see whether your heart is functioning well; ditto for electroencephalograms (EEGs) for brain function. Doctors take a long time to learn how subtle differences in these surrogate measures mean particular diagnoses for their patients.

Another way to make observations is by using measuring tools that can see what we normally cannot with our eyes. Anyone who has ever wondered how on earth a dentist can tell that a dark blob on an X-ray is a cavity knows how hard it can be to learn to read a type of image that isn't a normal photograph. For one thing, images like X-rays are not really pictures per se; they're *transmissive*, which means that things which block X-rays will appear bright (like bones) and things that let the X-rays through (like skin) will appear dark. A shadow is the simplest type of transmissive image – if light passes through, it's bright; if light is blocked by your hands making a dragon, then there is a dark shadow. A problem with transmissive images is that if, for instance, one bone is in front of another, the X-ray will show just one bright pair of crossed bones – not very useful if you are trying to see whether there is a crack at that very spot.

Other kinds of light we cannot see with our eyes let scientists gather data, too. We all have seen rainbows, which contain all the colors our eyes can see, from purple through blue, to green, yellow and then red. If we kept going off the red side of the rainbow, we would get to infrared light. Infrared energy is given off by just about everything – we cannot see it with our eyes, but we can feel it as heat if it is strong enough (another surrogate measure!). Infrared cameras show things that are warm as bright and things that are cold as dark. This allows scientists to measure temperatures of objects they cannot easily check with thermometers, like the tops of clouds. Infrared images of the Earth show clouds with cold, high tops in contrast to the warm ground or sea, allowing for good cloud images even at night. (By and large, higher cloud tops are colder, and probably imply bigger storms – more surrogate measures!) Infrared images of hurricanes and other weather systems allow meteorologists to make predictions that would have been impossible before the development of weather satellites.

Designing Good Experiments

Suppose you are lucky enough to be in a field in which you can do good experiments to determine how the world works. The word *experiment* brings up visions of bubbling beakers (and, in Hollywood, often maniacal laughter from a "mad scientist"). In real life, though, scientists have limited budgets and often experiments are expensive to do. Thus, it is pretty rare for someone in a lab to randomly try things to see what will happen. An experiment can involve months if not years of planning, not to mention a great deal of time finding someone to pay for it. Normally, scientists will spend a long time figuring out what question(s) their experiments will answer.

So how *do* scientists figure out what experiments they should do? A large part of science is posing questions. Very often, a good experiment will open more questions than it answers – and, to scientists, that's a good thing. To design that great, field-opening, Nobel-prize-winning (well, OK, science-fair-honorable-mention-winning) experiment, you have to figure out what you're trying to learn and why. The question you are asking ("Why did it snow more this year than last?") has to be posed in a way that can be answered concretely. It is also important that others can repeat the experiment and get the same result.

Different types of scientists have different problems trying to measure things when they do an experiment. For example, some types of physics experiments are very easy to do because our ability to measure relevant things is very mature. It is very easy to measure how much someone weighs at a given moment because scales are easy to manufacture accurately. However, pity the poor medical researcher trying to figure out whether a new diet helps people lose weight. Not only are there a lot of things that affect how much a person weighs, but the test subjects will probably fib about what they actually ate, might exercise more than usual because they will know they are going to be weighed in front of other people and so on. In other words, it is difficult in many areas of science (including medicine) to have what physicists would consider a *controlled* experiment.

A controlled experiment is one in which only one thing changes at a time and the thing that is changing (the *variable*) varies in a way that is understood as well as possible – hopefully in a way that can be measured accurately. If you've ever tried to get sound out of a silent stereo with a lot of control knobs, you can appreciate that it's hard to figure out why no sound is coming out if you change several things every time you try a new fix. Better to leave all but one knob alone, and try moving that, then go on to another, then maybe move a cable, and then turn the power on and off and start over. Scientists try to do the same thing, but sometimes it's hard to turn on and off only parts of the universe!

Biologist Charles Mobbs is a researcher at Mount Sinai Medical School in New York City. Mobbs studies the link between being skinny and living longer by studying mice, which get old and fat in ways similar to humans (although a lot faster!) and thus are a good *model* to use for studies like this. There are many factors that affect how long mice live, which sensitizes scientists working in fields like this to craft experiments very carefully. Mobbs says a good outcome is one from which you learn *something*, even if it's not what you had in mind!

Mobbs emphasizes carefully thinking through all the possible outcomes before the experiment starts. For example, he wanted to test a drug that might make mice lose weight (and, in the process, get some insight into how the drug works). First, he made some mice fat by feeding them a high-fat diet (doubtless the envy of their cousins gnawing out a living on the other side of their Manhattan laboratory walls!). Then he injected the drug into half the mice. The other half of these obese mice were instead injected with a chemical that he knows does not make mice lose weight. Mobbs asks, "But you might say, why do we have to do that? Why not just inject the drug into obese mice and see if they lose weight?" Many unlikely things can go wrong, though – the caretakers could forget to feed the mice, for example, which would make them lose weight. "Always do controls to pick up the things you didn't think of," he cautions.

The type of controlled experiment above is what is called a *negative* control – it helps analyze the cases in which the drug did work and makes it reasonably clear that it's not just some sort of accident that would have happened anyway. If the drug had failed to work, though, you might not have had enough insight to know why – did the drug not get to the part of the body where it needed to go, for example? Therefore, it's a good idea to have a *positive* control too. Maybe the drug should have worked but something went wrong. In order to rule that out, you would divide the mice into three groups, and inject one-third with the drug under study, one-third with something you knew did *not* make mice lose weight and one-third with something known to make mice drop those fractions of an ounce. No matter what happens, then, you would learn something – Mobbs' definition of a good experiment. He concludes: "Controlled experiments are built into the way that a scientist thinks. I couldn't do an experiment without a control any more than I could go to bed without brushing my teeth."

Having said all that, Mobbs continues, "In reality, though, you can't actually do a lot of science that way." Science can't really proceed without what he characterizes as "fishing expeditions" – casting a wide net to make some real progress without knowing how to do a thoroughly controlled experiment in a new research area. Since the experiments are not controlled very well, if you find nothing you may not learn a lot. If you *do* discover something this way, you can push a field forward in a hurry.

The classic fishing expedition example he offers is the discovery of the antibiotic streptomycin. A specialist in the biology of microscopic life that lives in soil, Selman Waksman got the idea that since mold lives in soil in successful competition with faster-spreading bacteria, mold must be producing a chemical that kills off competing bacteria. He sent his students (particularly Albert Schatz) off to various places to find mold that produced materials poisonous to bacteria. Finally, one day the group discovered one mold that killed off the bacteria that caused tuberculosis. This was important because other antibiotics available at the time could only kill certain kinds of bacteria (called *gram positive*), and tuberculosis was a different kind of bacteria called *gram negative* against which there was no defense. These fishing expeditions landed a big catch indeed – and saved many lives. In a somewhat controversial honor, Selman was awarded the Nobel Prize for the discovery, but many thought others who helped troll for the fish, notably Schatz, should have gotten some of the recognition as well.

Developing a Theory

The word *theory* has developed a somewhat different common meaning than the way scientists use it. For most people, *theory* and *guess* mean the same thing. However, to a scientist, theory is as high a level of certainty as is possible. Scientists are trained never to think of anything as absolutely correct (or not). They are trained to think of any body of knowledge as "the best information we have now" since it is their job to question and to move the line between what we do and do not know. Therefore, at any given time there are the best theories that constitute biology, physics and so on. There is nothing else – scientists cannot magically see a set of answers at the back of the universe's book! Therefore, they take their theories and continually question them to see how they can prove various parts wrong or incomplete and thereby move the frontier forward. This is the point that *is* alien to most of us – but is fundamental to science and is the point at which our looking-for-lost-keys example begins to fail us.

Scientists never feel they know an absolute, true-for-all-time answer about how some part of the world works. If they did, they would be out of a job! However, the best theory in a field has been questioned and tested and turned this way and that by the smartest people around. That means it is most likely right. Guessing, inventing other theories or otherwise developing completely new ways of explaining the world need to be tested in the same ways as the currently accepted theory – and any new hypothesis must be proven to explain the world better than the existing theory. Even better, a good theory has *predictive* power: We can say that if our theory is true, we can go out and look at thus and such and it should be a certain way. If that works out, our theory is stronger (and the new theory will supplant the old). Note that this requires a culture of openness, sharing of data and disclosure of limitations of any observation to work. It also means that no one has the ability or right to *declare* something true – the data and the observable world have to support the theory.

Somehow we have to guide experiments and all that data-taking. We can take all the data we like, but the exciting part comes when we can predict what the *next* data should be. Will it be a warm or dry summer? If we measure the number of birds along a stretch of coastline after wetlands have been restored, exactly how many more should there be ten years from now, and why? If we turn the biggest telescope ever developed on a particular area of sky, how many stars will we see? Scientists develop a hypothesis to explain things they have seen and to predict what they should see when they do new experiments and make new observations. A hypothesis, loosely speaking, is a scientist's best estimate about how things work, but it probably hasn't been tested yet by seeing whether it fits data that was not available when the hypothesis was developed. Scientists develop experiments or plan new observations to test and refine a hypothesis into a theory.

Some fields – like seismology, the study of earthquakes – have particular difficulties testing their hypotheses. California Institute of Technology's "earthquake lady" Kate Hutton is a frequent explainer of earthquake data on television. She says, "There is some experimental seismology – breaking rocks in the laboratory, etc. – but for the most part it is an observational science. You can make hypotheses, but sometimes you might have to wait a long time to verify them. One large branch of seismology is recording the best data possible, continuously, because, of course, we don't know the dates and times of future earthquakes. Another branch is piecing together the history of earthquakes from historic records or geology. Yet another is computational seismology, learning to model earthquakes and other phenomena on computers, thereby generating hypotheses that can be checked against the accumulated data." But, since earthquakes are (fortunately) few and far between, it takes a long time for any given hypothesis to be proven correct (or not).

Experiments in a Computer

Some scientists can use an animal to *model* a human being. Just like an architect creates a little model of a house before building one, scientists have a variety of ways to test theories when it is not feasible to experiment directly on their ultimate subject. For example, medical researchers like Mobbs use mice to test effects of drugs to avoid exposing humans to possible toxic effects. Even experiments on mice are usually approved by an ethics panel at the university or hospital in question, since no one wants to sacrifice any living thing without good reason.

The other way to test a hypothesis is to develop *computer models,* or simulations. Meteorologists, for example, take data all over the world and feed it into big computer programs that have been developed with the physics, chemistry and history of weather all over the globe. Data is fed into these programs all the time, and periodically new theories about how the oceans and atmosphere work (or bigger and faster computers!) lead them to be tweaked to be more accurate as time goes by. However, to build a computer model, the underlying science must be understood pretty well.

Forecasting weather depends on *computational fluid dynamics* (CFD) models. We understand fairly well what happens if we have a little cube of air and we heat it, add moisture to it and so on; most of that is physics that is easy to measure and analyze. What gets complicated is trying to understand what happens when you have a gazillion little cubes of air piled next to one another. The air is also being heated, cooled and humidified as it interacts with water, lakes, trees, desert sand and so on. What happens when one little cube of air has some sun heating it and another does not? Meteorology computer models divide the Earth's atmosphere (or a part of it) into many, many tiny cubes of air. Then, one cube at a time, these giant computer programs mix "real" data (from weather balloons, ground stations and so on) with predictions to forecast how warm or cold, wet or dry, each of those cubes is going to be, and whether wind and clouds will flow through them. Over time, steady improvements in computers (these babies take a *lot* of memory and processing!) as well as the ability to have robot measuring stations in more places have improved these models (and therefore improved forecasts). There are always a lot of assumptions, though, as well as things that have to be averaged and estimated to make it plausible to run these programs even on the biggest computers. Professional meteorologists usually run several programs (with different underlying assumptions, strengths and weaknesses) and then use their experience to combine the results into a forecast.

Once you have a weather computer model you believe, you can also use it as the basis of experiments. Suppose we are curious about how bad a storm five years ago would have been if the water in the Gulf of Mexico had been warmer. We can start out with a weather model and add more effects to it so that it can answer questions like this. These models, however, are only as good as the data and assumptions in them, and for something that models the entire Earth, deciding what to include accurately and what to estimate requires some deep knowledge of physics and other fields. Scientists can and do disagree about what it is important to include in computer models – disagreements that ideally result in experiments to measure the quantities in question, and observe how they vary and see the resulting effects on weather and climate when they do. Scientists have to spend a lot of time prioritizing what to go out and measure in these complicated situations.

For many sciences, however, we are still learning enough of the basics that we really can't yet develop a computer model, and we have to ask mice or yeast cells to stand in for us for a while longer. In all cases, though, a model is never perfect; but each model and experiment gets a little better than the last one, and gradually we learn more and more about how the world (or the universe!) actually works.

Science at All Ages

I am often asked to be a science fair judge. One of the things I find most intriguing about this is seeing how students go about learning the scientific method. Because of the limited science and mathematics young students typically know, projects tend to be oriented mostly toward experimental science rather than theory. All too often, though, science fair projects come off as something more appropriate for a cooking show: The process takes precedence over asking new questions. Yes, you can measure some quantity with great care – but you need to know *why* you are measuring it!   Nothing is more frustrating to a scientist judging a science fair than a well-executed project that appears to be an exercise in mixing chemicals with no obvious question answered by the student.

Good scientists spend a lot of time posing questions (and then spend more time trying to see if anyone *else* has already posed, and answered, this question, referred to by scientists as "keeping up with the literature"). I always get excited when a student has asked a good question, even if it is imperfectly answered. I get even more excited if I discover that they know they have an imperfect answer! With the internet, it is easier than ever to find background materials to answer novel questions. Learning to ask good questions and develop experiments to answer those questions is a key skill that is taught far too rarely. I try to start my young friends off as early as possible – all you have to do is let them ask questions!

Section 4

What Do We Do All Day?

The Big Picture

Relatives often ask me, "So, what exactly is it that you *do* all day?"

It's hard to describe within most people's attention span. After I fumble out an answer, the usual reply is "That's so nice, dear," and a change of subject.

First of all, what is the difference between *scientists* and *engineers*? The old joke is that a scientist likes to be surprised by unexpected results of experiments while an engineer does not. Scientists are explorers – sometimes literally, in the case of Antarctic researchers and astronauts. When a scientist uses and applies existing knowledge in novel ways rather than creating new areas of study, he may be called an "applied scientist" or sometimes an engineer.

To understand the difference between a scientist and an engineer, think about the difference between a research biologist and a doctor. The biology researcher spends a long time coming up with new questions, and might have a research plan spanning years. The doctor, on the other hand, has a patient for a few minutes, in which time he has to use all the existing knowledge in his field to develop a diagnosis. The researcher might find a cure for cancer and save millions of lives years in the future. (If that doesn't work out, more than likely he will learn something else and that will still be OK.)

Doctors usually have immediate responsibility for patients, and may be legally liable if they don't figure out what is going on. Scientists versus engineers have a similar split. Scientists pursue new knowledge for its own sake. Engineers have to know a wide range of current knowledge, and often need to figure out how to apply new knowledge generated by scientists. Depending on a scientist's or engineer's training and overall interests, the lines between them can be very blurry.

Often engineers are, like doctors, responsible for decisions that immediately affect lives and property, and they develop new solutions for problems on tight deadlines. Often engineers wish they could use things just discovered by scientists to do something new. More often than not, though – to avoid surprises – engineers have to go with what is known and has been used before, unless they are designing something that is impossible with current technology. Then, engineers and scientists have to talk to each other.

Science is fiercely competitive, and scientists sometimes find themselves underemployed (in the United States anyway) because of the lack of research funding and the specialization that makes openings in some fields scarce. The National Science Foundation (NSF) reported in 2000 that over the previous ten years it funded 30% to 34% of submitted proposals overall. Percentages are lower for younger scientists, so an early career scientist might have to write many proposals to get even one funded. Teaching typically covers nine months of an academic researcher's salary. The rest is found through grants or consulting. Academics must also obtain grants so that they can do high-quality research leading to publication in the science journals in their field. If they do not succeed, they may find themselves unemployed.

Even in a corporate laboratory, scientists need to convince executives that their research will bear fruit for the organization down the road. Those executives, in turn, need to predict the future: Do I believe this guy in the lab who might have a new product for our company in five (or 15) years? Will the new product cannibalize the market for our existing products? If so, are our competitors working on the same thing anyway and do we need to do this research to stay ahead of them? Researchers in this environment also have the disadvantage that, for competitive reasons, they often cannot talk freely about their work to their colleagues elsewhere. This tends to mean that corporate research and development labs need to be big enough so that there is a real community (if a partially closed one) for those scientists and engineers. Sometimes a scientist or engineer who fails to convince his employer that an idea is worthwhile will quit and negotiate to take some part of his research to start a new company, which then means the scientist has to talk to venture capitalists and other investors. Everyone has to agree what part of the not-quite-invented potential discovery the scientist owns and what part the former employer retains.

Science and engineering require tremendous focus and attention to detail. Many scientists are also talented musicians, since learning to play an instrument takes concentration, memory, ability to recognize patterns and sheer doggedness similar to that required in rooting through data, debugging computer programs or writing 50-page grant proposals. The sometimes-tedious leg-work behind great insights requires physical and emotional stamina. Keeping up with new developments is a never-ending task, and usually requires work in the evenings and on weekends – reading, talking to colleagues and bushwhacking through the forest of interesting new things that appear daily in all fields.

Science is similar to many other creative fields, in that people develop a small cadre of collaborators. Most science projects require specialists from several disciplines. Teams might be scattered around the globe, but modern communications (and the occasional airplane) hold projects together quite easily. In that sense, it's similar to the film industry. There, too, teams come together for the project and might split up and re-form years later for the sequel to a first success. A producer, director and writer might live in Los Angeles,

New York and Topeka, respectively, most of the time, but might go to live together in the forests of New Zealand for six months to shoot a film. Because it is relatively easy to make off with a new idea when it is being fleshed out, a culture of trust must develop, and peer pressure generally prevents theft of science ideas. Properly giving credit on published papers and patents, and recognizing who the primary inventor is, can accelerate (or wreck) careers. Both scientists and filmmakers are always raising money for their next project. In both professions, you're as good as your last success, and the quest for funding for the Next Big Thing takes up a lot of time that in an ideal world would be spent creatively instead.

Even though working with a group of people you know is comfortable, often it is necessary to graze the edges of other fields as well to find new paths. A new chemistry insight might have implications for biologists, and fundamental discoveries frequently jump across several disciplines. So it is not enough for a scientist merely to keep up with his own discipline, and new people must be added to a scientist's lists of collaborators over time. More than other scientists, field scientists depend on their logistics crews, pilots and mechanics. Even those who are working with more abstract ideas, like mathematicians, need to compare notes with each other or people in other fields.

Scientists tend to work long (and sometimes odd) hours, too. If a scientist is out in the field, he is probably more or less working all day – making measurements, packing samples and so on. Work in a lab might be driven by the process the scientist is exploring – if a chemical reaction takes 12 hours to complete, going home after eight hours isn't an option. If data on a biological process needs to be taken every four hours, often that means that a scientist (or assisting grad student) is going to be coming in every four hours, twenty-four hours a day, seven days a week until the experiment is done. Academic scientists usually need to teach classes as well, and scientists in industrial jobs might need to meet with colleagues in other departments. All in all, it tends to lead to lots of nights and weekends taking data or writing it up for others to study.

All this raises the question: Why would anyone become a scientist or engineer? The years of training are a big investment, followed by a life of long hours and a continual need to prove yourself. Most do it because they can't imagine themselves doing anything else. The thrill of exploration, and of seeing something for the first time, are experiences that can't be given up easily. All scientists share the explorer's drive – but use very different tools to survey their lands, literally or figuratively.

My career has been focused on helping teams of experts work well together. I sometimes say that I specialize in being a generalist, or a translator between people in very different fields. So rather than give you specific examples of things I've done I'll introduce you to a few very different types of scientists, throwing in a couple mathematicians and an engineer for variety. This will give you enough of a view so that you can imagine them working on your team every day, seeing just a bit farther than the day before.

Southern Crossings

I n their explorations, scientists push forward the boundaries of what we know. Sometimes this is physically, literally true, as is the case for David Vaughan, a British Antarctic Survey (BAS) scientist who studies the interaction between polar ice sheets and Earth's climate. Most of the time he is in Cambridge, England, at BAS headquarters. However, he has gone South, as they say, to Antarctica every three years or so since 1985.

Vaughan in particular has visited some of the more isolated areas of Antarctica, which explorers call the *deep field*. He says, "We do work pretty hard when we're down there. When you're out in the field it's the top of the logistics pyramid. We have the two bases and they're halfway up the pyramid getting things from the U.K. to the deep field." Because a lot of resources are expended to get to these distant places, once a scientist is in place, the workload is intense.

Is there anything – like certain foods – that polar explorers miss when they're in the field for months? "You get used to the food that you've got – all you want is food," says Vaughan. "You need the calories and you get that release from whatever you've got available. When you're out in the field with one other person for weeks at a time, it's pretty relentless. You're

so focused on that one job that there's very little real break. You have to find a release. For me it's reading books." A benefit of working in Antarctica in the summer, when the sun shines 24 hours a day, is reading in the tent at night without needing to put up a light. BAS uses reddish, conical tents that look like nothing so much as tepees from the American prairie. "I've spent many months over the course of years in those tents," Vaughan says, "a comfortable little womb in the middle of the white expanse."

In principle, Antarctica could have all 24 time zones arrayed around the South Pole, and sometimes this can create a lot of confusion. To give structure to the day, they schedule a particular time to call in to their base station. Usually they make this call the first thing of their day, and no matter how late they went to sleep the "night" before, they get up at that time and say, "We're going to get up and start a new day and call in." In many ways, these explorers have lives similar to astronauts on a mission.

What else does Vaughan miss? "One of the things that we look for in people we're interviewing is that they have to be able to handle *no* solitude. Your buddy is only going to be 100 meters away. If anything, it's quite a crowded space. You have to stay close to people. One of the nice things [about] being back in the U.K. is being able to walk out and not have someone on your shoulder. It's usually a good relationship, but there's always somebody there. And for ten weeks it might be exactly the same person." On his last trip to the Pine Island Glacier, on Antarctica's western side, he remembers, "We were nine people and we had sleeping tents, but our whole lives centered around one living tent and one science tent. Very much we were living on top of one another. We were out there for 60 days and we got very used to one another's company. It was a whole lot more sociable than going out with two people or four people."

Does Vaughan take accounts of early British explorers with him to read in the tents? No, he reads novels. Vaughan says that a couple of years ago, his expedition was attempting to get into Pine Island Bay. "We didn't get into Pine Island Bay because it was blocked by sea ice. When we came back, we were reading a book about Cook's expeditions. He probably got to almost the same point as we did. The explorers that went down there 100 or 200 years ago were so tenacious and so brave. I appreciate how tenacious and goal oriented [they were]. I find it very hard to read the accounts of what they did; it makes you feel very unworthy and small in comparison. The level of personal commitment is so much greater than what I can bring to it I find myself being embarrassed reading of what they did with so little. I tend not to read that sort of book when you're in the Antarctic. It's hard not to draw comparisons. These guys really did it. They laid their lives on the line just to explore. When they were down there the thing that must have pushed them on from day to day to day was not knowing what was there."

Landscape of the Mind

Exploring a glacier is one way to move back the frontiers of what we know. At the other extreme, the expedition occurs entirely in the abstract, using paper, pencil, brain cells and perhaps a computer. Probably the one scientific discipline we find the hardest to think about is mathematics. *Is* math a science? There are many types of mathematicians, ranging from statisticians who develop methods to understand whether bird populations are doing well in an ecosystem, to those doing very abstract work that might someday enable new ways of thinking about physics or chemistry problems. There are a lot of mathematicians. As one indication, the American Mathematical Society, a professional organization, reports 30,000 members. Many mathematicians are brought in as part of a larger team for their ability to propose ways to organize complicated problems.

But what does it all mean? If someone develops a new piece of mathematics, so what? Fundamentally, one can think of each new development in mathematics as a new tool that engineers and scientists can use to better understand and predict the world, just like inventing a new physical instrument such as a microscope. In the late 1600s, Isaac Newton and Gottfried Wilhelm Leibniz developed different mathematical techniques that collectively became what we call calculus. Calculus underlies almost all engineering work today, and there probably isn't an office building, car or airplane that didn't have someone using calculus during its design. A few hundred years later, the tools of calculus allowed pioneers to understand electricity and magnetism. Good mathematical tools can vastly cut down the need to hunt and peck around to find out how something works; a testable prediction can be made and a hypothesis proved (or disproved) using a mix of mathematical tools and shiny instruments. If you imagine how hard it would be to use just addition for your daily life without ever using multiplication, you can get the idea of how useful a full box of mathematical tools can be for people who use them daily.

Mathematician Niles Ritter points out the key distinctions between mathematics and the other sciences: "They call mathematics the queen of the sciences, but it differs from other sciences because it is not empirical. You can do mathematics completely in your head. Where's the world you're experimenting on?" Ritter has been a math professor and a researcher figuring out ways to process images from space, and now he's a problem solver for a software company.

Ritter continues: Imagine you had a cube from wire and you put it on the ground out in the sunlight. The wires of the cube's frame would create a complicated shadow on the ground. If an ant wandered by, it would not be able to tell that the pattern of light and shadow on the ground came from the wire cube above. When mathematicians solve problems that look complicated in two or three dimensions by thinking about them in more abstract realms, they call it *lifting*. Maybe a problem that looks too hard and complicated to develop mathematics for is a shadow of something that is quite simple in a higher dimension. Mathematicians think of the view from above – the broader view – as their world, in which the best understanding of how things work can be found. What is possible when mathematicians and others think *beyond* three dimensions? Mathematicians have a hard time developing good mathematics, for example, when something – poof! – changes from one thing into another. When a particle inside an atom splits in two, it gives mathematicians fits. Looking at things in higher dimensions lets a physicist look at the particle from a point of view as different as ours is from an ant's. Ritter allows, though, that this can tend to make mathematicians a little otherworldly!

If mathematicians create these worlds in their heads, how do they know that the cloth they are spinning has at least some threads tied to reality? Ritter notes that mathematicians have developed precise rules for understanding things. In the early 1900s, people like David

Hilbert tried to prove (using math) that some simple areas of math were completely consistent. After some decades of unsuccessful wrestling with this, Hilbert (and later Kurt Goedel) came up with *metamathematics* – theories about mathematical theories. He proved that even simple math could not be proven completely consistent. This continues to worry mathematicians, who have to depend on their own self-consistency for things too complex to observe in the real world.

How do mathematicians solve problems? Do they close their eyes and sit in a darkened room? Actually, one of the things they do is to talk to other people – sometimes other mathematicians, sometimes other specialists, depending on the problem at hand. If they get stuck, they might say to each other, "I've tried this and I've tried that," and another mathematician might tell about similar problems he might have seen solved a different way.

Mark Durst is a mathematician, and the executive director of systems informatics at biotechnology firm Amgen. His particular skill is framing a hypothesis precisely enough that the evidence at hand can be used to prove or disprove it. In a typical situation, Durst takes data another scientist has in hand and figures out what else has to happen to answer a concrete scientific question. He sometimes feels like he's building one side of the transcontinental railroad in the 1860s – starting from one place and hoping to meet his colleagues in the middle. "For me, there's a lot of making things up and seeing what some non-real world might look like," which in due course he can tweak until he gets a good enough model of the real world.

How does a mathematician know he's right? When he actually "does math" with a pencil and paper and symbols, Durst says, it's easy to assess whether he's right or not because the rigor of math allows two reasonable people to look at the work and objectively agree that one part follows logically from another. Scientists looking at data subject to interpretation have it harder. In biology or other physical sciences, a researcher may get to a certain point only to discover he can't take data to answer a question with current instrumentation, because the instrument isn't sensitive enough or there are other problems. It's also possible for tools to limit a mathematician, but it comes up less often. From the point of view of helping other scientists, mathematicians want to see if the math is "right enough" to provide data within a certain range. They then have to delineate when this kind of math will work without misleading results.

Why are people afraid of math? Learning mathematics is mostly learning how to think a particular way, which takes practice. However, as we discussed in Section 1, it can often be crucial to find a good coach so that your practice is effective. Problem-solving specialist Niles Ritter's opinion is that most people could be mathematicians, but phobics had a bad math teacher who did not understand mathematics. Math phobics develop a picture in their heads that math is like a ladder. Down at the bottom rung is learning how to count, and then the next one up is multiplication, then algebra and so on. Not a good picture, he says; math is much more an art rather than an empirical science. There are as many different kinds of mathematicians as there are artists, and different mathematicians will develop different problem-solving styles.

There are some mathematicians who think visually, and others who think about the exact same objects in a verbal way. To solve the same problem, one person might immediately go to a whiteboard and draw a sphere, circles and so on to get a feel for how the problem might appear if physical objects were interacting. Someone else would do nothing but draw letters, symbols and arrows. It's like drawing versus writing to explain an artistic idea. But in the end, they're all abstract – and all mathematicians love the abstract and the ability it gives them to lift above the real world and fly around, looking down on us mortals and helping to solve our problems.

If I am helping someone with a math problem and they get stuck and start hyperventilating, I ask: "*If* you knew the answer, what would it be?" Amazingly often, people will answer that question with the *correct* answer, given the implied permission to be wrong. To learn a discipline like math or science, you must be willing to try things and fall down sometimes, just like an athlete learning a new move. Durst, for his part, finds that when he knows instantly how to proceed it's often because he has followed the analogous false tracks in other areas many times. He's good at recognizing patterns, which he applies, for instance, to finding things in other people's kitchens. This sort of skill, though, takes lots of practice! Mathematicians have a certain amount of faith that if they try enough avenues they will ultimately find answers, but there sure can be a lot of crumpled paper in the meantime. The reward at the end – knowing that you have the unambiguous correct answer – is a powerful motivator.

For the Birds

Earlier in this section, we met a scientist who explores a literal frontier, and a few who work in realms that are more abstract. Even the discipline of biology encompasses a huge range of topics and styles of problem-solving these days – from analyzing DNA down at the scale of molecules to understanding entire ecosystems.

Dave Moriarty, a professor of biological sciences at California State Polytechnic University in Pomona, sits between these extremes. He studies why certain species of birds live together while others aren't in a particular community. He says, "That tells us about evolution, about how the world came to be the way it is. On the more practical side, it tells us about conservation. If we want to save something we need to know the rules about its assembly." There are some bigger questions out there right now about how birds are related to other species on Earth. For example, based on unique features shared by bird and dinosaur skeletons, some scientists think birds are really dinosaurs. (Further evidence is that birds and a certain kind of dinosaurs called theropods are the only creatures known to have feathers.)

Moriarty's research group at Cal Poly studies birds and their habits using a combination of statistical analysis and fieldwork. One area that has received a lot of attention lately is how birds elect to set up house-keeping. DNA evidence has allowed scientists to establish the paternity of chicks in a nest. This has shown that the prevailing theory – that most birds are monogamous – is not necessarily true. Sparrows will form a seasonal pair bond and build a nest, but there is a fairly good chance the babies weren't fathered by that male – even though both parents are engaged in caring for the young. "Theory," he says, "has fallen behind the empirical evidence." To catch up, more fieldwork is required to get more data about how things work.

Mist nets (which Moriarty describes as "a hairnet gone wild") are set up to catch the birds without hurting them. The nets are taller than a person, about 12 meters long and arranged in a way that resembles four shelves. The nets are black and normally placed where vegetation is thick. Birds fly into the nets, and researchers such as Moriarty's grad student put bands on them. With the bands in place, Moriarty says, "She could recognize who was hanging out with who and take a blood sample." When the babies hatch Moriarty's student also takes samples from chicks. If she finds eggs broken she tests DNA from the eggshells as well; because birds have lots of predators, there are lots of broken eggs. Blood samples are analyzed back in the lab with more or less the same technology used by crime labs to develop DNA profiles. She will also keep track of how many chicks are female and how many are male to see if any population imbalances occur. Over time, this new data will give us an understanding of how bird populations evolve in an area, and how to protect populations when changes due to natural or manmade causes disrupt a bird's environment.

Moriarty guides many budding scientists through their studies. Some may become employees of federal or state fish and game agencies. Those students learn how to do fieldwork, and also have to learn how to do a lot of background research on both what is known about the animals they will manage and their habitats. They have to know about current laws protecting the creatures they are studying, and might have some work to do getting various permits before grabbing the binoculars. A developer may want to build 50 houses at a particular location and need biological surveys done. Scientists trained by Moriarty might be assigned the task of doing the survey to see if any state or federally protected birds, mammals, reptiles or amphibians would be affected by the development.

How is Moriarty's area different from other scientific disciplines? "The scale of the problems is quite different," he says. "We're interested in chemical processes but want to know how it plays out at the level of organism." In other words, he tries to find the big picture of an ecosystem in the DNA of a bird's egg.

Good Chemistry

C hemistry is probably the discipline that is the closest to the stereotype of science, bubbling test tubes and all. What do leaders in the chemistry profession think about how they are perceived? I decided to ask one highly decorated lab denizen for his views. Michael Marletta is a professor of chemistry, biochemistry and molecular biology and chair of the chemistry department at the University of California, Berkeley and, to boot, a member of the National Academy of Sciences (a prestigious group of about 2000 scientists that is often asked by Congress and other public agencies to weigh in on policy issues). He's a former recipient of a MacArthur Foundation "genius grant" and has a list that goes on forever of his various activities and honors. Despite that massive resume, Marletta took the time to plop down on a hallway sofa at a San Francisco scientific meeting to enthuse about science in general and chemistry in particular.

The American Chemical Society, not surprisingly, calls chemistry the "central science" because chemistry solves problems in other disciplines. For his part, does Marletta think chemistry has an image problem? He says, "Chemical spills, accidents, cost of fuel, environmental problems [are all] laid in chemistry's backyard.

When these chemical plants blow up or there is a nuclear plant accident – that's [perceived as] chemistry's fault." There's no question, he says, that there are times when chemistry *was* at fault, but, in his view, chemistry is also inextricably linked to everything good. If the stereotype isn't really correct, what do chemists actually do? One answer is that they often work very closely with scientists in other disciplines – these days, frequently with biologists.

Marletta, who often has worked in areas with combination titles like "medicinal chemistry," says the current division of science into its traditional academic departments pretty much was set in medieval European universities. The problem, he says, "is we never told nature that's how it organizes itself." A question in biology about how some biological process really operates at some point becomes a chemistry question. "My own chemistry," Marletta says, "has always had an adjective in front of it because biological problems can be solved using chemistry." His focus is the chemistry used by biological systems: "I realized that's the chemistry I wanted to understand: How does biology do that?"

Marletta emphasizes that the commonality in all science is to explore. How does he decide what terrain might be the most interesting? "If I had two problems," he says, holding his hands about two feet apart and looking from one to the other, "how would I measure which one was better?" He says that part of his emotional makeup is that discovery is great and science is wonderful, but he would also like it to help people. His group at Berkeley is studying some of the chemistry of the parasite that causes malaria. I asked him how he had decided to chase that particular problem. Before his malaria work, he had chosen research projects based on trying to discover some new fundamental aspects in biochemistry, to look at a slice of nature at the level of the molecules composing it. His motivation for looking into the mechanisms of malaria, though, was a little different. When his first child was born, he stepped back and decided to re-examine how he should pick problems to solve. One influence was the realization that his then-infant son might not live long in parts of the world where infant mortality was high. This led him to become interested in parasites, such as *plasmodium falciparum*, cause of the most severe form of malaria. Malaria infections are present in 300 to 500 million people a year, and kill one to three million a year, according to the Centers for Disease Control. Marletta's website reports that 85% of those who die are children.

Marletta says that parasites do weird things because they live inside another organism, a host. Over the eons they stop doing some things that an independent organism would do. The malaria parasite, *plasmodium*, lives for part of its life cycle in the blood of its human victims. It consumes a substance in blood called *hemoglobin* for breakfast, lunch and dinner. Hemoglobin in turn contains a molecule called *heme*, toxic to many organisms. Marletta wondered, "So how do the parasites get rid of heme?" Asking that question has led him down a variety of interesting routes. He and his students are still exploring whether a drug could perhaps interfere with plasmodium ditching the heme the parasites ingest, with any luck poisoning the parasite and thus curing the host. Even better, since humans don't have to get rid of heme the way plasmodium does, side effects should be minimal.

What are some other big problems coming down the road that chemistry, in partnership with many other disciplines, will solve? Marletta thinks developing biofuels is a crucial area where chemistry will play a key role. Why is this an interesting chemistry problem? Plants have issues: They live outside all the time, depend on sunlight and are stuck where they are if a predator comes along. They deal with that, he says, by making themselves sturdy, stable and unappetizing to predators. What people working on biofuels want to do is to take plant material and break it into useful chemical pieces, but it is hard to do because of the plant's evolved defenses. There are organisms that do it – for example, white rot fungus. However, the fungus has no real evolutionary pressure to grow fast, so using its methods takes too long to be industrially useful. Termites, too, are not very efficient at breaking down the cellulose in wood – they are also (fortunately for homeowners) very slow. The teams working this problem will need to come up with novel ways to beat out the fungus and termites with a faster process.

Beyond getting past the stereotypes, nonscientists need to understand the technology options chemistry creates. Policy decisions in areas like biofuels require educated policymakers and citizens. Chemists and their teammates from other disciplines might invent the best energy technologies in the world, but the average consumer and the companies that serve them have to feel those solutions are safe, cost-effective and reasonably convenient. The chemistry required to make those reactions go forward might take a while to develop.

Robot Crew

W e have covered a range of types of scientists – and even had a foray into mathematics! To complete our tour of different kinds of scientists, we need to ask: What does an engineer do? In the introduction to this section we laid out some of the differences between a scientist and an engineer. What does an engineer who considers himself a researcher actually do all day?

An associate professor of engineering, Chris Kitts rides herd on undergraduate and graduate students – and robots. The robotic inhabitants of his gizmo-stuffed lab space have been to the bottom of Lake Tahoe, to trenches off the California coast, to innumerable places on land and sea, and even into space. Floor to ceiling whiteboards at his Santa Clara University lab, located in California's Silicon Valley, are covered with diagrams, scribbles and to-do lists, a reflection of the frenetic activity that almost never seems to slow as students raised on video games move on to controlling a machine in the real world. Developing and building these robots teaches Santa Clara engineering students how to design and build a complex machine. It also teaches them to work in teams to create something bigger than any one student could possibly make. This is a crucial lesson to learn for their professional careers, since most engineering projects require teams, sometimes with thousands of participants.

Kitts and his student crew can provide low-cost exploration services to scientists. For example, the *Triton* remotely operated underwater robot has explored the depths of Lake Tahoe, allowing scientists to see what they think might be evidence of ancient landslides. (We will learn more about those discoveries in Section 6.)

For Kitts, the difference between engineers and scientists is simple: "An engineer's ultimate goal is to build stuff." Sometimes that means working in an environment very close to that of a scientist – determining how feasible new technology might be without necessarily aiming it at concrete problems. Engineering research gives those who are oriented to solving specific problems more tools and options. Kitts, like so many others in this book, believes that "tinkering" is the key to getting kids excited about science and engineering. Hands-on experience lets students go through the whole process of hypothesis testing and allows them to go off on their own tangents. Is tinkering enough? No, he says, "a next crucial step is catching it up with the real engineering analysis." Tinkering, in short, works better if you know what you're doing!

Scientists and engineers help each other explore new ideas. Scientists develop fundamental knowledge, which lets engineers design new and better things. Sometimes those new and better things are robots that let the scientists explore further and develop new fundamental knowledge. In the last few centuries, this cycle has tightened and accelerated, with both benefits of and problems caused by technology multiplying rapidly. Will the explorers be able to find new solutions as fast as technology's unforeseen consequences multiply? Our next section will talk about how scientists see themselves, and the consequences of their discoveries, in bigger social contexts.

Section 5
Scientists in Society

The Evolution of Science Activism

When I was growing up in the 1960s and '70s, science was an honored (and presumably honorable) profession. However, in the '90s and 2000s I have seen a gradual shift in public attitude. Science and scientists appear far less unambiguously positive. Scientists routinely defend their new findings to their colleagues in normal give-and-take scientific debate. Often they now also have to defend the entire process of doing science to a broader audience. Most of us thought that the debate about whether or not the scientific method works had been settled hundreds of years before. Evolution, climate change, cloning, stem cells – areas that only a few years before would have been discussed by scientists at specialized meetings – were suddenly political issues, soundbitten and sensationalized on television news.

Like many scientists and engineers, I was initially perplexed by some of these discussions, particularly in the area of the accuracy of Darwinian evolution. In science, truth and evidence eventually prevail, and most of us presumed this would be the case and the whole thing would blow over in a few months. Darwin developed his hypotheses, tested them against observations and published his resulting theory in 1859. As we discussed in Section 3, a theory stands the test of time if its predictions can be tested in new ways as technology enables more kinds of observations. The predictive power of Darwin's theory – developed long before DNA was even a concept – has been astonishing over the last nearly 150 years. DNA evidence allows scientists to discover how closely related different species are, and to look back in time to determine the branching of our family tree eons ago. Genetic techniques (as well as evidence from geology and other fields) have strengthened Darwin's case over time.

To the surprise of many scientists, belief systems that were religious in nature began to paint themselves as "science" to the point of inserting new and untestable material into science curricula. A scientific theory has to always keep itself open to testing and so is never "proven right." Rather, it is carried by scientists as the best knowledge we have right now, until exploring the world gives us more knowledge. Religion, on the other hand, usually requires that its believers take on faith a core belief set that does not change over time. This means that these two ways of looking at the world are not comparable. This doesn't mean one has to be wrong if the other is right; it just means that one cannot solve science problems with religious methodology, and vice versa. It is crucial in science that everything be testable and open to question to be considered scientifically verifiable.

This dichotomy was presented by the anti-evolutionists as: Science is uncertain about its accuracy whereas religion is not (with an implication that certainty was good). It was further used to imply that science was hostile to religion. It took a while for the scientific community to realize that this impression was spreading through large parts of the population in the United States, and that literal interpretation of the Bible and Darwinian evolution were being weighed with the same scale. There have been many good websites and books written on this topic as well as on the broader issues about whether science and religion are (or are not) compatible. I particularly like the views of Father George Coyne, until 2006 the director of the Vatican's astronomical observatory. Father Coyne has given many interviews in which he talks about how he reconciles being a Jesuit priest and a scientist, and delineates the circumstances when he feels it is appropriate to use the scientific method and when to use faith. I've pointed out a representative selection of materials on these topics in the Resources section of this book. My focus here is on how this turmoil has affected the public's view of scientists, and scientists' view of their role in social policy and education.

Many scientists operate in a realm in which they deal, for the most part, only with other scientists. My personal observation is that this can cause deep misperceptions about the "average person's" view of science. Therefore, many in the science community were surprised by how widespread the attempt to discredit evolution became (and remains today). To scientists' frustration, some people who don't buy Darwin's theory point to the word *theory* as reason enough to dismiss it, choosing to define *theory* as something akin to wild notion rather than in the scientific sense of hypothesis that is confirmed by everything we know so far. As a result of that debate (as well as other controversies, like climate change, covered in several other sections of this book) scientists have had to become more vocal and organized, and learn to communicate more effectively with the public. They want to be certain that scientific points of view come from scientists.

One of the negative science stereotypes that made things worse was the impression that scientists are aloof and amoral, if not downright evil. Scientists are portrayed as uninterested in their work's social implications. In practice, most scientists I know spend a lot of time wondering about how what they're doing makes a difference in the bigger scheme of things, and hope that they are adding to the body of knowledge that so far has made each generation's life a bit easier than that of the one that went before.

By the nature of their jobs, some scientists, such as those who work for public agencies, are faced more immediately with the impact on others of decisions they make. They continually apply their training to serve the public's interests. However, "the public" is composed of many individuals and groups, each with their own sets of desires and priorities. This section will focus on scientists who make difficult, science-based decisions every day that affect ecosystems and lives. As a counterpoint to those who have careers in public service, we will meet one engineering professor who tried to learn lessons on building better office towers from the World Trade Center 9/11 events, and found himself at the center of conspiracy theories. Finally, we will meet a psychologist who works to understand how to explain science to us in times when it is important to be right. These stories, taken together, will give you a feel for not just how much scientists want to *know* – but also how much they want to be sure that their knowledge makes a difference, now and perhaps centuries from now.

Voices of the Endangered

Science careers can be all-consuming. As a result, a scientist might find himself explaining to his wife why he needs to make a late-night foray to count rare toads splashing down a rain-lashed road. Some avoid these explanations (or, more likely, lengthen them enormously) by marrying another scientist. Husband and wife Bob Cook and Mary Hake, currently working at Cape Cod National Seashore in Massachusetts, have made studying and advocating for endangered species their collective life's work. Cook is a wildlife ecologist for the U.S. National Park Service; Hake, a biological technician. They live with their 10- and 14-year-old daughters far enough out on the Cape that just a couple of miles of land separate the Atlantic from Cape Cod Bay.

The rhythm of Hake's life is driven by the migrations of the piping plover, a small, endangered shorebird that nests on undeveloped beaches. The birds return to Cape Cod from their winter migration around St. Patrick's Day, leaving in late August or September. She works the six months a year that the plovers are in residence. She says, "It's perfect for my life and the balance of my life. We both couldn't work constantly and have the kind of life and atmosphere we wanted to bring up the kids in." She has the best of both worlds, she says, being able to both spend time focusing alter-nately on the plover's chicks and her own.

The six months the plovers are around, though, Hake is as frantic as she would be during a visit by a picky houseguest. The plovers lay their camouflaged eggs on the sand, vulnerable to being accidentally crunched by a visitor's foot (or dog). So, the first step is to fence off the beach each year with what Hake calls symbolic fencing – just a line of string intended to warn people off, but not actually to stop them. Once the plovers start laying eggs, "there are never enough hours in the day," Hake says, because birds along 20 miles of shoreline need protecting. Once the eggs are laid, she places wire boxes over each nest, open on the bottom and held down by stakes pounded into the sand. These predator exclosures have openings large enough for an adult plover to come and go, but too small for foxes or larger predatory birds. No subtle, expensive instruments here: Hake's tools are a shovel, chicken wire, stakes and a sledgehammer, which she wields with impressive gusto.

Just as important as the aerobic part of her job is her presence on the beach in a National Park Service uniform, explaining to people why they need to keep their dogs away from the plover nesting area. She realizes that she might only have one to three minutes before people lose interest and wander off. If the time of year is right, she will show them a plover chick: "If someone has an off-leash dog I show them how vulnerable that chick is." Once they see an actual cotton ball of a chick, she says, their dog will be on a leash thereafter. "We'll get an injured gull on the beach and 20 people will gather around it," she says, but since the plovers are out of sight, a chick killed by a dog doesn't get the same sympathy. Hake says that it's important not just to inform people about rules, but also to empower them so that they know they can make a difference.

Hake says her greatest frustration is the small number of visitors who resist her attempts to protect nesting plovers. (The extreme version of this attitude manifests itself on local cars sporting bumper stickers that read "Piping Plover: Tastes Like Chicken.") She understands the importance of educating the public but realizes that if a person is 50 or 60 years old, their attitudes are harder to change. "But that doesn't stop me from trying" she says. "I do change some and it's so rewarding," as when local kids excitedly tell her about how they are watching out for plovers. "That's what makes our salary priceless."

Cook has a more traditional year-round job, as a PhD scientist developing reports and statistics about the Cape's fauna, with stints before that as far away as American Samoa. His is far from being a desk job, though: It can involve going out on rainy nights to close one of the park's secondary roads to protect the spadefoot toad (listed as threatened by the state of Massachusetts). Rainy nights are a particularly good time to collect information on the number, sizes, ages and sexes of the toads brought out by what they apparently regard as fine travel weather. "What I end up doing," Cook says, "is collecting pilot data on subjects of interest that may have bearing on management issues." This data can be used to entice graduate students from universities to come and do a more thorough project for their thesis, and spend more time than realistically he can on any one issue.

How do Hake and Cook think about the need to save species? They don't really think of it in those terms. Cook says that that in the national parks, "We're trying to preserve not necessarily individual populations or individual species but the ecosystem and ecological processes that go with it." Cape Cod, for instance, has various rare environments, such as its deep freshwater kettle ponds, salt marshes and the like. The reality, though, is that as soon as you build roads and parking lots in a national park you have impacted natural processes within the park. Even when the environmental judgments do not involve people, difficult management issues can arise. For example, Cook says, "We have a habitat that was altered 100 years ago that one group of people are trying to restore, but the complicating factor is that some state-listed rare species are making use of that habitat in its present condition." To decide what to do in cases like that, he would consider how abundant the two different competing species are within the park. He might expand his analysis beyond the boundaries of the park to a regional and state level, taking into account lots of factors.

"The truth is, with landscape management, any decision you make to do something, even if the decision is to not do anything, is going to affect some population." If you have a species that builds nests in fields, over time wild fields will become shrubs and then woodlands. As the land goes through succession, it is occupied by one group of species and then by another. You might have to decide to sacrifice the field species to save woodlands, and your decision would depend on other fields and forest and how much of each remains available to any rare species.

Are all species created equal, then? For wildlife biologists like Cook and Hake, they are. However, for the general public, big furry animals that can't be missed when they stand in the middle of the road command more attention than, say, bugs. (Animals with a bit of cuddly factor advantage are referred to as "charismatic megafauna" by biologists, with a bit of tongue in cheek.) Cook points out that most animals are small and spend most of their lives hiding because otherwise they would be easy pickings for predators. For the extreme example of this, imagine the lot of the endangered bug. Cape Cod, for instance, has an endangered species of beach beetle, which occupies the same habitat as piping plover. It can be a hard sell to convince people who want to use vehicles on the land that a beetle and a small bird need saving as part of preserving the larger ecosystem.

Why are Hake and Cook spending their lives working to keep these creatures alive? Why not let endangered species die out? Cook says he wants to prevent extinctions caused by the impacts of industrialized human beings. There are pragmatic reasons for this since sometimes a plant or animal has medicinal or other immediate value, and extinction cannot be reversed. Beyond the pragmatic, though, says Cook, for many people there's a spiritual and inspirational reward in being able to see animals and plants in their natural habitats rather than relegated to a zoo. "Ultimately, the long-term survival of wildlife is not going to be based on squeezing the last animal out of a piece of land. It's going to be based on educating people about the effects of their lifestyles on the natural world." He hopes that people will become more aware of population growth's effects so that they will make wise decisions about housing and transportation that are harmonious with the land. Perhaps the couple's work will someday result in a world in which, as he puts it, "wildlife isn't relegated to something that's only in preserves but wildlife is part of the world wherever one lives."

Predictions

S cientists can work on various aspects of weather prediction: They can be out in a forecast office, giving predictions daily, or they can be researchers who focus on improving the tools of those who are out there making forecasts. Weather forecasting, like any other scientific activity, is based on observation and theory. The predictions made by interpreting its underpinning theories get tested very visibly every day, with potentially great impacts to life and property. The National Weather Service has forecast offices scattered around the country, usually with two forecasters per shift. The offices are staffed 24 hours a day, seven days a week, and typically cover an area of a couple of dozen counties.

Dennis Feltgen is a National Weather Service meteorologist and public affairs specialist, communicating with the press and public about weather events. Talking to Feltgen makes it clear that weather forecasting is a good microcosm of science itself: Many things are known, but, as he says, "There is still more we don't know about the atmosphere than we do." Forecasters' science knowledge, experience and judgment have to fill in the rest. What is a National Weather Service forecaster's shift like? The first event of the day is normally a briefing by the previous shift. Then the new shift becomes responsible for the station. The forecasters now settle in to give themselves what Feltgen calls "a little situational awareness." They look at measurements taken in their area, data from satellites and radar, and how the weather might be changing. There are also big computer programs that are run at the National Centers for Environmental Prediction in Camp Springs, Maryland, that produce forecasts. Different computer models predict some things better than others. Thus several models are run a few times each day (and can produce results different from each other, which is where the human judgment comes in).

Feltgen says that experience is a huge factor, since forecasters who have been in a particular office for a while learn local patterns. He says that everyone says their weather is weird. Any given locale will have its own quirky patterns due to terrain and the like. Thus, local experience with what has happened in the past with a given set of circumstances can provide crucial insight if the rest of the information is contradictory. Forecasters will compare notes with surrounding offices too. Feltgen gives this example: Let's say the Miami forecaster says it will be a really wet day, but the forecaster in Melbourne, Florida, to the north, says it's going to be dry. Forecasters will then coordinate with surrounding offices so that strange jumps in weather aren't predicted at county lines!

Feltgen explains that a typical forecast office is staffed by at least two people: a lead forecaster and one who focuses on aviation forecasts. The aviation forecaster might also work on the long-term forecast (four to seven days ahead), or the marine forecast. If severe weather is anticipated, more staffers will be brought in to manage the work.

What is it like when you do your first live forecast? Feltgen says that people are walked into the job gradually. "You are trained along the way. It takes a while to work up to the forecast desk."

How does a forecaster balance the hazards of making a storm prediction that is too alarmist versus the hazards of not being alarmist enough? Feltgen was with the forecast office in hurricane-prone Key West, Florida, for three years. During that time, the area was affected or threatened by a number of storms. He says that a forecaster gradually integrates the seriousness of the situation into his products as time goes on. Keeping reports factual reflects the seriousness of the situation while avoiding panic. In the case of hurricanes, in particular, the National Hurricane Center in Miami has the responsibility of issuing watches and warnings about where the storm is going. After that, the weather forecasters in the affected areas create the hurricane local statements, a much more detailed and definitive product. Feltgen says, "The idea is to get that info out to everybody." When he was a Key West forecaster, there were no local television stations there. So, he developed a web product that got out detailed information for that area. Can scary weather affect the forecasters themselves? He says he never had to actually bail out of the forecast office in severe weather, but they did have a plan, just in case. (In Key West, the plan at the time was to evacuate to the local county jail!)

There is another type of forecaster called the incident meteorologist. There are about 120 of these specialized meteorologists who can go on site where a dangerous situation is unfolding. One of the most common is forest fires. Feltgen explains that an incident meteorologist has a little satellite-based system that will pull in data and very specific forecast information for the site, particularly about wind, humidity, temperature and rain. These specialists work long hours and are instrumental in fighting fires. Since the work is so intense – it can be 16 hours a day – they are rotated out every couple of weeks during long-running problems.

How often do they get the weather right, and how can they tell? Feltgen says, "We're always verifying our forecasts." What was the actual temperature? What was the average wind speed? Another meteorologist's dream is more data about weather over the oceans, since weather everywhere is very interconnected and we do not have the kind of data over the ocean that we do on land. Feltgen would also love to have even faster supercomputers to run the weather models in more detail. The bottom line, though, is that forecasting the weather still requires a lot of research. When I asked Feltgen what he would say to someone considering forecasting as a career, he said, "If you're looking for a job where you're going to be perfect every day, this is not the job for you." That might not be a bad description of what it's like to be a scientist in general, either!

Conspiracies

Sometimes scientists and engineers inadvertently find themselves part of a public debate. In September 2001, Eduardo Kausel thought his MIT students should learn something from the collapse of the World Trade Center towers. As he watched the 9/11 attacks on New York unfold, he wrote down some of his thoughts. Kausel, a professor of civil and environmental engineering, started to develop his own analysis of what must have happened. Then, as he passed his class notes around, his colleagues started to add other ideas. Soon, the MIT press office had put their work out on its website as an independent view, done purely from professional interest, of the events of 9/11. From there, Kausel says, "It snowballed" with calls from media throughout the U.S. and Europe.

To his surprise, he was soon being attacked for broadly agreeing with the official reports on what had caused the Trade Center buildings to fall. The key area that he had analyzed was whether, amid a hot jet fuel fire, steel would begin to weaken and ultimately cause the collapse. The Trade Center buildings had been designed to withstand the impact of a 707, guarding against a lost plane heading to nearby Kennedy Airport rather than one deliberately flown into the building. Still, people asked, why the collapse? His analysis showed that a jet fuel fire could in fact weaken steel enough so that it could not hold up the building – the steel would become "like chewing gum." The fact that the towers stood for a while and then collapsed worked with this hypothesis for him: Initially, they *did* stand after an aircraft impact. It was the fire that then weakened the steel and caused the failure a bit later on.

Why the reaction? As his analysis circulated on the internet, the difference between "weakening" and "melting" steel was ignored. Steel weakens and softens at a far lower temperature than that needed to actually melt it. A group styling themselves as "academics" (mostly in disciplines far from building design) put forth a hypothesis: Since the high temperatures caused by a jet fuel fire was not high enough to melt steel, then there must have been explosives placed ahead of time in the Trade Center towers. Furthermore, "the government" must have placed these explosives. The leaps of imagination here (and confusion about Kausel's actual point that steel weakens significantly at the temperatures produced by burning jet fuel, whether or not it is hot enough to melt) are immediately seen as problematic by anyone with scientific training. Just the same, in 2006 he still was receiving about one email a week from people wanting validation of their conspiracy theories. Why the fascination and why is it so persistent?

Could it be that people really do not distinguish between science and fiction, and lack an appreciation of whether something is likely or not? It's easy to read, say, Dan Brown's novels *The Da Vinci Code* or *Digital Fortress* and begin to believe a single thread of extremely unlikely logic. The error of logic that occurs is that people forget that just because something is proved not to be white, that does not necessarily mean that it's black. Kausel is concerned that schools are not preparing the populace for a world based on scientific facts; rather, people believe just anything. The scientist's mantra "Based on what we know now it appears that..." comes across as indecisive.

"The public at large doesn't understand how science operates," says Kausel. Scientists make their theories stronger by looking for contradictions and things that don't fit. However, for many in the public, "They already have decided [what to believe] and anything that contradicts that is dismissed." Kausel calls this *"reverse science* – choose what you want and dismiss what you don't like." Certainly, this isn't a good basis for learning what went wrong in the Trade Center towers – and what to do better in future. Somehow, scientists and engineers have to get across that not all answers are right, and that the scientific method is still the best way we know for picking out the best set of knowledge.

What You See Is...?

We have met wildlife biologists and a weather forecaster who have to get information across to the public quickly. We've met an engineer who got information out to the public and found himself part of a less than perfectly informed debate. Is there any way for scientists to improve how their message will come across to the public? William Hallman, director of Rutgers University's Food Policy Institute, studies how to do just that. Hallman, an experimental psychologist by training, determines how the public perceives risks by understanding what mental pictures people develop based on information they get from informal sources in their lives.

What does Hallman think the key differences are in the way a scientist and a nonscientist think? Of scientists, he says, "We filter information and we tend to be more numerate than the rest of the public," and "we pay attention to more of the details." Scientists are immersed in the scientific method. If a scientist writes up a paper that lays out his assumptions, hypothesis and conclusions, anyone who disagrees with any part of that should be able to articulate some reasons why. Hallman says, "Implicit in that process is the assumption [that] by repeating the methods we should always get the same results and reach the same conclusions. The problem comes when the lay public doesn't reach the same conclusions, the scientist concludes that the lay public is irrational because [the public] can't be convinced." The second part of this, he says, is that the response of the nonscientist public to this is: "I laid out my argument and the scientist wasn't convinced, so there must be something wrong with them."

Hallman says that there are three parts to explaining a scientific discovery, from the public's point of view. First, who are you and why are you doing this? Second, how does it work? Third, what does it mean to me? The natural tendency of a scientist is to lead with and describe in detail the second point – how it works. However, most nonscientists don't care. They want to know the first and third points: What was the scientist's motivation, and what does it mean for me? Problems can arise when there is no clear societal consensus about what problems are worth solving.

"I'm a psychologist," says Hallman, "and I study public communication of risk." He talks on topics like health effects of electric fields and lead poisoning. When he speaks at science conferences about public views of these issues, usually someone will say that science education is awful, and if we could just get people to understand the facts they would reach the same conclusion as scientists. He calls this making the public into "mini experts." He feels, though, there's too much to absorb and scientists can't teach the public enough in every field. Hallman points out that we wouldn't expect a physicist to know enough about DNA to make a good decision about genetically modified foods, but are disappointed when the public cannot.

Hallman works by surveying people with open-ended questions that force them to describe how they think about a scientific field, rather than giving them questions with multiple-choice answers. For example, he surveyed people about their understanding of cloning. He says that people are surprised to learn how advanced cloning is. They remember Dolly the sheep and wonder what happened to her. He says respondents, "Can't quite remember – 'Jolly ... Folly ... Molly ... that sheep they cloned.' They often will confuse cloning with stem cells." They imagine a cookie cutter or giant copier spitting out full-grown animals; they know the end product but have no idea how it all works. Hallman says, "You know what? People don't really care all that much. It's not that they don't want to know. They do want to know *why* you're doing the research, *who* is doing the research, do they look like me, do they think like me, would they make the same decisions as I would? Do they trust the scientist to do what's right?" The public focuses on outcomes and consequences: What does this mean for the animals involved? What's the problem that it solves? Will there be intended and unintended consequences? All this is considered by the public in the framework of whether or not this violates their sense of ethics and values. Scientists, Hallman says, start every discussion of cloning with how it works rather than the questions above that people care about.

What advice does he have for scientists? He says to imagine explaining what you do to an interested but uninformed audience, such as your mother (assuming mom is not a scientist too!). Fortunately, there are scientists (and journalists) who are trying to meet in the middle of this divide. In the next section, we will see what happens when scientists and journalists try to communicate with each other, and then with the public at large.

Section 6

Should You Believe
What You See and Read?

Read Carefully Before Investing

I f you had money to invest, there are certain publications you would read for advice. You might or might not act on your friend's stock tips, based on your perception of his expertise (and net worth). We accept that we need to research and to evaluate our sources before investing money for the future. However, investing money isn't the only way to plan ahead. Consider this: What individual or group is in charge of long-term planning for your health and welfare? Who is thinking about what global environment you, or your children, will have to live with 20 years from now? Whom would you trust to make those plans? I would propose that the science community fills that position. Therefore, when planning your future, you need to consider scientists' input as carefully as you would that of your investment manager.

To effectively know how to use science information in your own life, you need to find good science news coverage. News outlets often report science in superficial "bites" or only in the context of a controversy, leaving in-depth writing to publications that specialize in science. Casual newspaper readers or TV news viewers are left thinking all developments in science are either controversial or giant breakthroughs (or both) with little insight into the broader context. Scientists, in turn, fear the nuances of their work will be lost if they talk to a reporter. They steer clear of the mass media, choosing instead to write articles themselves in the specialized journals that cater to other scientists. In these publications, they can be certain the details will be correct and no reporter will intrude between them and the public. These journals, though, are not meant for the general public. This leaves a big gap between the professional science publications and the mass media.

Often, science stories involve statistics, which are easy to misinterpret and difficult to explain well without the full context of a science journal article. One area where I find this particularly problematic is in medical reporting. We might get excited that a breakthrough has occurred if we read that a new drug cuts the risk of heart attack in half for black women ages 65-74, with seven percent of drug recipients having significant side effects. Cutting heart attacks in half with a small percentage having problems is good, isn't it? However, when we analyze this and do a bit of digging, we get a different view. According to the American Heart Association, 13.8 black women per 1000 have a first or recurrent heart attack each year. Therefore, if you gave a representative group of 1000 black women this new drug for a year, you would expect to eliminate six or seven heart attacks. What about the side effects suffered by "only" seven percent of patients? Seven percent of 1000 is 70: This would mean that 70 people suffered side effects to eliminate six or seven heart attacks! A better measure is the *number needed to treat,* loosely defined as the number of people who have to take a drug for some specified amount of time before it is likely that one of them will see a benefit. It's rarely used, though, presumably since it does not lend itself well to catchy headlines about cutting risk in half!

On the other hand, suppose some new strain of flu was said to be likely to triple flu and pneumonia deaths of children age four to 15 in California compared to 2004. This news might cause panic, a run on flu vaccine and a lot of money being spent to prevent these deaths. However, the California Department of Health Statistics says that just eight kids in that age range died of flu and pneumonia statewide in 2004 – so even tripling still means tiny numbers, at the scale of California's 2004 population of 36 million people.

Beyond numbers misrepresentation, how many ways can science reporting be misleading or distort the facts, even if what is reported is accurate (if incomplete)? If the reporter has no science background, it may be difficult for him to decide key questions to ask and to pick out the most crucial parts of the interview responses a scientist has given. This is particularly a problem if the scientist doesn't make the big picture clear up front. A lack of perspective can cause a minor problem to blow out of proportion, create controversy where there is none or miss key points. A reporter might miss subtleties and caveats, or push for black-or-white answers when all the supporting facts remain fuzzy and grey. Sometimes, too, a story will give equal weight to several sources, some with an understanding of the science at hand and some with little or none. When science affects public policy, science can become entangled in politics and corporate or academic self-interest, which can lead to distortions, omission of facts, partial reporting of a story and other issues.

Even if the original report is in a specialized science magazine, a mass media outlet like a big-city newspaper might pick up on the story and condense it. Further, the newspaper's reporter might ask for comment from people who are not the right technical experts and then publish a far different story than the original (often, for a bigger audience than the accurate original, too). Next, the Associated Press (AP) wire service, which produces stories of widespread interest for hundreds of member newspapers throughout the country, might write its version of the story, which would be even shorter and might have different comments. Both the newspaper and the AP might post the story – radically condensed and possibly altered in context – on their websites. Then a television station or network might broadcast yet another version of the story, and also post shortened versions on their websites. Over time, the results can drift significantly from the reality.

Myth vs. Reality

O ne example of a story that took on a life of its own was the "face on Mars" myth. In July 1976, the JPL Viking spacecraft was orbiting Mars. It took some of the best pictures at the time of the region of Mars called Cydonia, notable for some rugged terrain. The JPL press release that went with one particular image had the unfortunate phrasing: "... the huge rock formation in the center, which resembles a human head, is formed by shadows giving the illusion of eyes, nose and mouth." Media outlets picked up the story with differing degrees of embellishment. Groups rallied around claims that the feature had to be artificial in origin.

Later spacecraft, with better cameras, captured images from various angles showing that the original face-like image was an effect of light and shadow. To this day, there are still advocates talking up the alien origin of the terrain – usually claiming that the later (sharper) images were doctored to hide "the truth." Experiences like this make scientists become much more precise and much drier in their delivery of results, which unfortunately gives the image that scientists have something to hide (or nothing of interest to say!).

To fight off exotic misinterpretations, a scientist needs to talk about his research and sound certain enough to be believed (yet poetic enough to be interesting). This is particularly an issue in the early stages of a research problem when all aspects of a discovery are inherently rife with open questions. Scientists who desire to inform the public about the implications of their work have to struggle with the balance between their training to lay out all possible objections during their discussion and the public's desire for "the answer."

When listening to a debate it is natural to believe the protagonist who makes unequivocal statements versus a scientist who lays out all the uncertainties and areas yet to be explored. If someone says, "My mother had cancer, we gave her a Chinese herb and she was cured. Therefore the herb must work better than all that fancy radioactive stuff," it is very hard to counter that anecdotal argument, particularly if you want to believe it. Just the same, it is necessary to study whether or not the herb actually helped and, if so, how broadly the results might apply.

Predicting Earth's Climate

We have just seen how an innocuous piece of science data (a picture of Martian hills) can be blown out of proportion and into alleged proof of an entire alien earthmoving operation. After a while, a preponderance of evidence will allow most people to easily conclude that indeed that area of Mars is not an ancient city. Journalistic problems often arise, though, when there are science issues that require more subtle expert interpretation than this. How can you, as an intelligent consumer of the media, detect the difference between a true scientific disagreement in which new knowledge is being sought to answer questions versus individuals with no knowledge of the field creating a "controversy" that the scientific mainstream knows is without merit? Let's examine climate change, a universally significant and complicated topic that requires us all to be intelligent consumers of information and opinions coming from many sources.

Forecasting natural events like earthquakes or the future climate of the Earth is a giant undertaking, requiring scientists to think about effects encompassing hundreds of millions of years and tens of thousands of square miles. *Climate* is defined as the very long-term trends in weather in various regions – for example, right now Southern California has a climate that is hot and dry in the summer and cool and wet in the winter. That doesn't mean there might not be a warm, dry day in the winter – climate refers to long-term trends, not day-to-day weather. The current climate debate centers on how much people's actions affect Earth's climate. For purposes of our consideration, let's distill this very complicated debate down to one between those who have a strong interest in the status quo trying to present data that minimizes mankind's effects on the Earth and those who stand to benefit from change doing the reverse. How can we get a big picture of where the most likely road to the truth lies?

The best tools scientists have now to develop long-range climate predictions are adaptations of computer programs developed to predict weather, paired with observations of how the world is changing (and thereby validating, or not, the predictions made by these computer programs). The polar regions' growing or shrinking ice coverage shows the effects of climate change more dramatically than temperate climes. Thus polar researchers act as a sort of early warning system.

One of the oldest and most respected polar scientific exploration groups is the British Antarctic Survey (BAS). What does the director of BAS, Chris Rapley, say of the best way to inform the public about what the polar regions are telling us? Rapley says that what really separates science from anything else is that a scientist is able to make predictions based on known facts. This, he says, is where the extraordinary power of mathematical science emerges: Inexpensive computer power allows us to build entire virtual worlds in a computer, using real data as the starting point. However, any computer model has assumptions buried in it, and so even when these reflect the best scientific consensus at the time, often holes are picked in the results based on the weakest assumption. Says Rapley, "In a way the numerical models have provided a sort of Achilles' heel" for those who want to dispute predictions of climate crises. However, he notes, in many cases the problems appearing in the Antarctic are apparent even with calculations carried out on the back of the proverbial envelope.

How does a scientist like Rapley evaluate evidence of climate change? The best evidence is to be found in the layers of snow that fall year after year on the polar regions. In the coldest places, this snow persists year-round and builds into ice sheets kilometers thick. The layers left behind vary in thickness from year to year, with chemical compositions of the ice (and any trapped air bubbles) depending on worldwide conditions at the time. This thick blanket of snow builds up over millennia, with layers visible if a section is lifted up out of the ice. A technique known as *coring* has been developed in which a machine drills down into the ice and scientists carefully cut out a long, thin cylinder of ice called a *core*. By keeping careful track of which core segments came from how deep down, a great deal of information about the Earth's weather for thousands or millions of years can be read from these records. Furthermore, bubbles of air dating back to those long-ago winters can also be trapped in the ice and analyzed to see how the air differed then from its current makeup. Over time, other records – in the layers built up at the bottom of the oceans, for example – can be cross-checked with the polar cores and, after a while, a preponderance of evidence begins to be obvious.

Rapley shows people of various stripes ice core data so that they can draw their own conclusions. He says, "We start to show them ice core evidence. About half an hour into this one of them will stop us and ask us, 'You guys really believe in this, don't you?'" Rapley finds their wording very frustrating, since he sees cores as hard evidence, which does not require a leap of faith. However, since some background is needed to understand that evidence, it can sometimes *appear* to be based on a belief system to those without the requisite years of training.

Rapley sighs at how hard it is to get the public to take up a call to action. "The message at the end of the season is that climate change is serious and potentially dangerous, and climate change is now. What do you do about it? That's where it gets difficult. What we're missing are the instruments for global collective action. People have known for long enough now that smoking is bad for you, but still smoke." He explains that if you stick your finger in a fire you know you are hurting yourself immediately, but smoking appears at the time to be a net booster of mood and the negative effects are far in the future. Rapley feels international leadership is needed to get the world to take action on such long-term and sweeping problems, but thus far his message has not entirely crossed into the policymaking world.

Rapley feels recent policy events show that it is insufficient just to build a reservoir of knowledge. In the late 1990s, Britain's government funding sources expected that publicly funded research would realize science's social potential without any real interaction with politicians. Funding was set up to keep politicians at least one step distant so that they could not tell scientists what to do. Now, for British scientists at least, "The contract with you goes further than that. You are expected to hold a dialogue with the general public about what you do, and you will contribute to the U.K. or public life." It is important, Rapley says, that the general public see science as accessible, and for scientists to contribute to that accessibility. "Stick to your science, communicate it clearly, and it is fundamentally powerful. It is bound to win. Unless people are so ill-motivated that they are determined to deny the truth, [science] will win." I hope Rapley is right, but motivations in this area are complex and the financial implications are vast – never a good combination for unbiased data reporting.

Science organizations have become more conscious of the need to produce position papers for the public (and legislators) on key issues like global warming (see the Resources section of this book for examples). For a long time the science community was not motivated to engage in policy debates, a situation that is changing rapidly. In the United States, various science groups have arisen (or changed charters) in the last few years to, for example, defend the rights of scientists in U.S. government jobs to speak freely about such issues as climate change and the status of endangered species even if the scientific truth goes against government policy.

Why should you bother to keep track of the facts about climate change and scientists' recommendations about climate change and similar issues? For one thing, it is an area that may have huge lifestyle and financial impacts on all of us. If, for instance, the sea level rises significantly over the next few decades, low-lying coastal cities will feel immediate impacts – and so will you, if you pay an insurance premium, own property in those areas or face tax increases to cover the affected public infrastructure and services! Science policy decisions, like decisions about traffic light timing or haircuts, are things we only tend to notice if the results are unpleasant. In areas like climate change, we may not have much time to act to avoid tragic results down the road – and the planet, unlike an ill-considered buzz cut, might not be able to grow back. So, just as you'd find a financial advisor to figure out where to put money for 20 years, reporters covering experts like Rapley can make it possible for their readers to participate in the discussion about how much risk we want to take with Earth's climate now – and 20 years hence.

Dispatches from the Frontier

A big part of finding good science information is to find outlets and reporters that you can trust. (The Resources section at the end of this book offers a list of magazines, websites and the like to get you started.) One reporter whose track record I admire is Leonard David, a senior space reporter for the website *space.com* and its affiliated print publication *Space News*. He covers a beat ranging from NASA missions of all stripes to small aerospace startups. To aerospace professionals like me, this seems like a huge territory; to a mass-market newspaper editor, it seems like specialization. In any case, he has the luxury of really knowing many of the key players in the field. His laid-back attitude and affinity for plaid shirts makes it seem that, for him, it's the most relaxing thing in the world to interview a CEO or an astronaut.

What makes for good science reporting? David doesn't hesitate: "I do think it all comes down to the onus [being] really on the reporter to know something about the topic they're writing on. I know this stuff and I've been doing it for a long time. So I'm in an odd position of growing up with writing about space and having an opportunity to meet the people who are making space happen." Although it's possible to talk to people on the phone and produce a story, it's important for him to see people building and testing spacecraft. Otherwise, the human side of the technology gets lost, and the story sounds like the spacecraft built themselves. When I worked in the spacecraft arena, I found that often people assume that any kind of engineering – for that matter, anything involving math! – is tedious. David tries to counteract that stereotype by reminding his readers that building spacecraft is not a dry exercise but "people doing this for people."

David finds it best to do his homework and get comfortable in that world of the scientist we talked about in Section 3, where special words, even whole languages, are developed to describe a project or the entire discipline. "It's a challenge to talk to an engineer who is acronym-heavy. I'm partial to getting in there and knowing acronyms ahead of time. For me, it's fun." He sees this as a way to demonstrate reporting know-how to the scientists. "I really try to make them comfortable that I at least know what their project is." It's essential, he says, to do research (just like the scientists he interviews) to get an original story, versus waiting for press releases to appear.

How does he choose his subjects? "Sometimes I'll write an article to educate myself. I'm usually receptive to odd things." Yet he tries to stay sensitive to the interests of his readers. What happens, though, if reader interests drift too far from reality? David notes that frequently he is asked frustrating questions by the public such as, "Did they really land on the moon?" Or about the face on Mars. The tendency for people to want to believe in government conspiracies and cover-ups is strong, and he wonders what drives such suspicion.

How does he avoid overstating a discovery? "I'm fond of asking people, 'Tell me what you don't know.' If you can get to the point where a scientist will tell a writer about what they don't know, then you tell the reader it's not a done deal. Particularly kids need to know there's open-ended exploration going on here." On the reporter's side, he says, "There are times when any reporter should say, 'Hey, I don't get it.'" Asking the question several different ways can help: "Sometimes it takes me three or four times."

David would love to understand how great inspirations and the scientific method work together. Where do those flashes of insight come from, in between long stints of testing or using data? It's not something anyone can really articulate, and those unexplainable, unpredictable flashes often lie at the core of a great story.

David suggests that scientists have to fight the human tendency to think of "the media" as one homogeneous beast. He points out that scientists need to remember that reporters from the trade magazine *Aviation Week,* which reports on details about spacecraft components, need completely different information than a reporter from a magazine with a title like *What's Up Lately*. One of the issues with scientists talking to reporters is that scientists have to pitch their message to the right level for the outlet – difficult when, more often than not, it's not an outlet scientists read or watch. (For example, I watch perhaps two hours of television a month – so I have to ask for information about the intended audience if I'm talking to someone doing research for a TV show!) Like science itself, it all comes down to asking good questions until the answers start to appear.

The Balancing Act

 Hline

How should scientists handle publicizing a discovery with the potential to cause panic, or at least to topple property values? What is their obligation to publicize risks that might materialize with serious consequences – or might not? Should scientists wait to achieve some sort of consensus before they talk to the press outside their own community, or should all of us see debates in progress? Given that the general media might not understand or convey the nuances about these uncertainties, when should potential risk be made public?

Those hypothetical questions became very real for Richard Schweickert, a geologist at University of Nevada, Reno, when he found evidence suggesting that powerful tsunamis might have once surged across Lake Tahoe – raising the question of whether they could possibly happen again.

Schweickert has devoted most of his career to understanding how the *crust* – the thin layer of rock that makes up the top 25 to 60 kilometers of the Earth – has evolved, particularly the thick crust under the Sierra Nevada mountain range in California and Nevada. Now, he is weighing the risks of what to say in public about possibilities in the future of Lake Tahoe, a large lake lying in that mountain range with a shoreline heavily populated by hotels, casinos and all manner of expensive real estate.

"I'm a field scientist," Schweickert says, describing his work gathering data about the makeup of the Earth – including the part that lies beneath the cold, deep blue waters of Lake Tahoe. To explore the bottom of Tahoe, he needed a robot that could take pictures down there – commonly known as a *submersible* – and Schweickert didn't have one.

He happened to meet Chris Kitts, director of the Robotics Systems Lab at Santa Clara University (and profiled in Section 4), who soon sent around an email saying that he was going to take Santa Clara's submersible down on an exploration of the bot-tom of Lake Tahoe, and scientists who wanted to par-ticipate were welcome to help out. The two, together with colleagues, have since gone exploring three times, in the spring of each year, before the Tahoe waters have too many boaters that might interfere.

The robot, Schweickert says, can get close to the bottom and look at side cuts of lake, just as a human driver might examine a section of road cut out of rock. If the robot does a systematic search – for example, a series of traverses back and forth from deep to shallow water, like mowing a lawn – it can map many of the features currently under deep water, such as faults, landslides or types of sediments.

"We discovered some features that were very puzzling. In shallow water near Tahoe City, there were boulders, spatially arranged into these east-west uniform ridges. They were about fist-sized all the way up to two meters. Some process has taken random boulders and put them into ridges. We had never known that until we did some traverses."

This raised questions: How were they formed? What process could take boulders that could weigh several tons and arrange them in these parallel rows? "We thought about as many possible ways as we could," he continues. Could glaciers have floated off the peaks that ring Tahoe and left the rocks behind in what geologists call a *moraine* (a rubble pile at the edge of where the glacier melts)? No, he says – any place cut by ice would have deep canyons, and Tahoe's bottom, near Tahoe City, does not have those. In addition, the height of the ridges is lower than glacial moraine would be. "We just ruled that one out. That left us with the other hypothesis: that some large powerful waves might produce what might be called mega-ripples."

Features like the ridges of boulders on the bottom of Tahoe have been seen a few other places: in Montana, in western Washington and in Hawaii. In those places, the features appear to have been caused by enormous floods and tsunamis. So, since no other explanation seems to fit, should we conclude that at some long-ago point huge waves whipped across Lake Tahoe, driving freshwater tsunami waves onto its shores? Could it happen again?

"The question about future risk is a very charged question," Schweickert says. "As scientists we're stuck with this dilemma about having concerns about the hazard, but we are trying to find ways to present this information [to the agency that manages Tahoe]." He says he has to be careful to understate his concerns to the public: "I've given a number of talks, but I try not to get into too much speculation."

What would it mean if there might be a tsunami risk around Lake Tahoe following a nearby earthquake? Several active and well-known faults lie beneath the surface. "People's time for owning a house and geologic time are different. Maybe these things only happen every thousand or tens of thousands of years. The probabilities are low. At the same time, there should be some awareness of what could happen. Management and emergency organizations could have a plan for worst-case scenarios." If one is balancing risks and resources, he notes, "There's a far greater hazard of wildfires."

Schweickert says, "The scientists have an obligation to share the information they have. But, somehow, you have to step back – definitely a balancing act. I am very cautious when speaking to the press." How does he communicate uncertainty? "That's a difficult one. In geology we commonly say: 'We can't tell you the probability of how long before something happens. But we can say if it did happen, it could happen.' There's no reason to think it won't happen in the future. But are you willing to take a chance that it won't happen for 10,000 years?" He suggests that we assess risks of living in a particular area by noting the experts who live in this region. If they live there, that is a statement of their perception of the risk!

Meanwhile, what would we need to consider if we wanted to try to minimize the risks of a tsunami splashing over the sides of Tahoe – just in case? "Before mitigating, we'd have to know more about the properties of the lake sides, what would make them fail.... We need more research. Is this a 100,000-year event?" At the moment, though, competing priorities have resulted in this work being minimally funded – and, for now, Schweickert is presenting his work to other scientists to get their opinions on what else might have put those boulders in rows on the bottom of Tahoe.

We can (to a degree) predict weather because there is a tremendous amount of data. A "20 percent chance of rain tomorrow" is based on the experience that, when conditions were predicted to be those expected tomorrow, about 20 percent of the time there was measurable rainfall. Unlike the continuous parade of weather, though, there are only a handful of earthquakes (and even fewer subsequent tsunamis) in human memory in any given place. This means if anyone uses the scientific method to make a prediction, it might be a long time before the prediction is validated. It's a very different thing to validate that it will rain tomorrow versus proving a prediction that an earthquake will happen in a particular area some time in the next 10,000 years!

Reporting for the Mass Media

D avid Perlman is one journalist who has followed the Lake Tahoe research. Perlman, longtime science editor at the *San Francisco Chronicle*, interviewed a colleague of Schweickert's for brief stories about the Lake Tahoe tsunami risks in 2005 and 2006. The headline on Perlman's 2006 article gave me pause: "Surprising Find Beneath Lake: Underwater Slide Kicked Up Tsunami, Geology Shows." Despite the headline, the story did convey that there were still some uncertainties in exactly what was going on under the lake. Various news outlets subsequently picked up the piece. This headline on an Associated Press version of the story is a rather unequivocal "Lake Tahoe Landslide Caused Ancient Tsunami." Based only on the feedback he has received, Schweickert believes that overall the exposure for the issue seemed to be a good thing, with people interested but hardly panicked. For Perlman's part, he says that he can't work for a San Francisco newspaper without thinking that anything having to do with an earthquake is a story.

I asked Perlman how he decides which stories to cover (other than earthquake topics) considering his newspaper audience is so diverse. First, he says, he will cover something he himself is interested in – hoping "that people will be interested in the things that intrigue me or puzzle me or excite me." Then he asks whether the story has anything to do with the lives of people in his readership area. Perlman says it's rare for legitimate scientists to call him or email him and say they've just discovered something; typically, they publish in the peer-reviewed journals first. (For example, the 2006 Tahoe story in the *Chronicle* is careful to note that the story will appear in depth in the upcoming issue of the scientific journal *Geology*.) Therefore, he routinely reads the major science journals and leans on them heavily to get ideas for stories. Since Perlman has been a science journalist for decades, he can usually think of someone he trusts to run an idea past if something comes in from an unconventional direction.

What advice would he give someone wanting to evaluate an article? "Consider the source," he says. If it is a controversial subject you can check that the reporter has given due recognition to both sides of the controversy, and read between the lines to see whether the reporter has a hidden agenda or bias. Unless you have time for further research, though, it will be diffi-cult to distinguish genuine controversy from the trumped-up variety – so your choice of reporter or media outlet must be made carefully. One option might be to go to the websites of three national newspapers, say the *New York Times*, the *Wall Street Journal* and the *Los Angeles Times*, and compare how their reporters present a story the days it breaks. Perlman says as a particular theory gains evidence and momentum he feels it is not necessary to show a side that has been surpassed by evidence. For example, in 1964 when the U.S. Surgeon General produced an early definitive statement on the link between cigarette smoking and lung cancer, he and his colleagues also called up tobacco company researchers and got their take on the situation. Now, he says, the link is so well-proven that he does not feel there is any further need to routinely include the opposing view. He thinks that global warming – and humans as its cause – are also now so well established that it is no longer necessary to include an opposing view in those stories.

Perlman worries about the public's image of science, and particularly kids' image of it. "Science is science and politics is politics and religion is religion," he says, alluding to debates over evolution and other topics that try to blur the distinctions between those three realms. He finds it frustrating when readers ask him how he "really knows" something; he is dependent on what the scientists in the story believe is true or present as fact (and, of course, his own choice of scientist). In the end, what makes good science reporting? Perlman says curiosity and intense interest in the topic are crucial, as long as the writer is capable of good, clear reporting.

No matter how good the scientists' explanation and the reporter's exposition, though, sometimes readers do not read stories carefully. Perlman recently wrote a brief piece about experiments done to explore whether a particular type of wild wheat might have some valuable nutritional features. He was careful to say that although various genetic engineering techniques were used to *analyze* the wild wheat, new strains bred from it were developed using conventional cross-breeding techniques. He says, however, that he received emails condemning him for promoting genetically modified organisms – even though the article was careful to point out that the wheat in the food chain was being bred traditionally. Every day, he tries to get across his stories, but everywhere in the chain that ends with the reader there is a possibility for misinterpretation.

Preaching to the Choir

There are publications that specialize in reporting science to the public, and in particular there are ones scientists themselves turn to for information. How do those publications maintain their quality? George Musser, an editor of the well-respected magazine *Scientific American*, says that evaluating competing science claims requires work. A scientist, he says, has to be comfortable with uncertainty. "People see science as a provider of answers, which is fair to some extent." This involves evaluating evidence for and against new discoveries and new ideas to pick out the best known "answer" at the moment. When asked how he reviews something new, he says, "For me it involves first a process of being a student and researching something, and asking a lot of questions if I don't grasp something immediately. I'll say, 'Explain that to me again, or … here's an aspect I don't understand.'" What makes science is that anyone should be able to reconstruct the result.

To evaluate a controversial claim, Musser tries different approaches. He will wait a little while and see how consensus develops. He asks: "Who's done it and have they been their own best critic?" If the scientists have not worked through all the possible things that could be wrong with their new idea, they may not have caught the problems. The thing that frustrates him the most about science reporting in the general media is a tendency to be "google-eyed and gee-whiz." This tends to reduce any analysis to a minimum, and makes it easier for a dubious idea to gain some traction before it can be examined and discussed by experts. Is working through public misperceptions worth it for a specialty magazine? Musser thinks so.

"People ask me who the greatest competitor of *Scientific American* is, and I tell them it's apathy. It's passivity." He feels that just about any question – even a hostile one – is better than a lack of interest. "When people write in to the magazine with questions, a lot of them are saying between the lines, 'You know, that's interesting. I want to think about this more.'" For him, it's not about an initial reaction to an idea, but what they do with it later. The one thing that drives him crazy, he says, is if someone passively accepts or passively rejects what he is told – the "whatever" response. Musser draws an analogy with his own reaction to art and music. "I'll say, 'I hate that painting.' Then later I begin to think and it provokes me" to think and learn more. Passivity, on the other hand, makes it impossible to progress and to change. He also thinks that the internet can "close the loop" between a reporter and audience, which can create discussion and make misperceptions more clear.

Even though Musser has science training himself, these are lessons that can be used by everyone: Look at the source, look to see if someone asserts they are right without proof, and see if they question themselves. It's your future that you're planning – be certain you have the most facts before you invest in it!

What's It to You?

W e have now seen how an incorrect interpretation of data can grow like a weed (the
Face on Mars); how two scientists (Rapley
and Schweickert) think about telling their stories to the
media; and how three professionals try to do the most
complete job of reporting. How can you learn from this
to be a better media consumer? A common thread in
these stories is that it is important to find out what
scientists themselves are saying (and to determine
which sources are indeed scientists themselves).

If something sounds outlandish, consider the
source: Was it a magazine that specializes in science?
Does the scientist have a website, or is he giving a public talk near you? Media outlets perceive that the public
is not interested in science and that undiluted information is "too hard" for the average person. Prove them
wrong by subscribing to science publications or attending a public lecture at the nearest university (most universities have a link on their websites that says,
"events" or "news" or "lectures") – look at those from
time to time, and consider getting your science undiluted.

What about online resources? Although some internet science resources are good (and free!), don't assume
that just because a website claims to be the voice of an

"institute" with a director who is "a PhD" that it is a trustworthy science site. The PhD might be nonexistent and the "institute" address a post office box. For that reason, I usually suggest to people that they start their search at a known point (for example, a web page at the chemistry department of a well-known university). Then, other sites linked from there are probably good sources as well. Sources that link *to* a legitimate site, however, might or might not be legitimate themselves because there is no easy way to police links into a site. For similar reasons, I usually hesitate to suggest use of Wikipedia except as a broad starting point for research, since there is no guarantee that a qualified scientist was the last person to edit a particular entry. The Resources section at the end of this book lists some well-known publicly accessible sources of good science reporting, but it is not meant to be exhaustive. The main advice I would give is: Slow down! If you hear something that doesn't hang together and it's important that you get it right before you change your diet, buy a new kind of car or take other important action – see if one of the suggested sources also reports the new result, or at least try to find this new information more than one place. Read the science stories in your local newspaper, and see if certain reporters seem to cover stories you care about – and, as suggested above, compare how different major newspapers covered the topic. If you feel strongly about a story it is always possible for you as a consumer to contact a reporter yourself: These days, most reporters' emails appear alongside their bylines.

Just as you would for any kind of advice, take a little time to review reports of discoveries that will directly affect you. How many people are making the claim? Who disagrees? Is key information left out, particularly if some statistics are quoted? What are the motivations of the people making claims? What does it mean to you, one way or the other? A little extra thought or digging now might make a big difference to you – and to others on the planet – years, or even millennia, down the road.

Section 7

Looking Back, Looking Forward

Looking Back

L ast summer I had an opportunity to visit the town of Plymouth, Massachusetts, where the Pilgrims landed in 1620. Even though it was June, it was chilly and rainy – one of those New England early summer days when all you want is a bowl of chili and someplace dry to eat it. There's no shortage of such places in the tourist part of Plymouth, but it seems only right to earn your food and warmth by walking around for a while first.

Plymouth's waterfront looks out onto Cape Cod Bay, a chunk of the Atlantic protected by the curve of the Cape. The water on this drizzly day was flat under a low gray sky. A full-scale replica of the *Mayflower* rests in the harbor, absurdly small and with the odd bit of plastic sheeting covering parts presumably under repair. (What would the Pilgrims have given for a big plastic tarp, one wonders – not to mention outboard motors?) A little way around the curve of the shore, there stands an enormous mausoleum-like edifice. In the middle of its imposing grayish columns there is an opening in the floor. I peered through the columns and down the hole, and discovered that all this structure is designed to frame a bit of rippled beach and Plymouth Rock. The memorial is wildly out of scale for what is left of the Rock after nearly 400 years of erosion, tourists and other insults. Perhaps it should be, given all that has unfolded since the Pilgrims' buckled shoes first stepped here. ·

I decided to walk up to higher ground to look out over the city and the bay. I went up past the tourist shops and restaurants, past the church, and found I was walking uphill into a wooded graveyard. The only sound was the trees dripping from fog accumulating into drops on the branches, and my footsteps on the path. I paused where a sign announced I was standing at the grave of the colony's leader, William Bradford, and looked out through the nearly illegible mossy nubbins of tombstones, the misty trees and wisps of fog that closed out the bay below. It was easy to imagine the early days of the colony, with black-clad figures making too-frequent trips up this hill.

What would Bradford make of me? What would he make of my airplane trip in five hours from Los Angeles to Boston? Would he approve of my time working at the Jet Propulsion Laboratory on robot spacecraft that sailed alone to other planets? What would he think about a United States with nearly 300 million people in it, and cures available for nearly all the common diseases of his time (but not for some new ones)? What about Massasoit, the leader of the Wampanoag tribe living here then? What would *he* make of me? Statues in town honor both men, and it was not hard to imagine either of them walking out of the mist to ask me what my business might be: Bradford in his black "Pilgrim hat" and swinging cape, Massasoit for his part wearing a breechcloth. I imagine showing them spacecraft images of Saturn and Venus, and telling them what we now know about those places. Even photographs would be surreal for them, much less images captured by a robot flying on its own to other planets.

What would Bradford and Massasoit ask me? If they saw a tourist bus go by on the road below, would they think the world had been taken over by witches and was now run by magic? Would they ask if people still had wars and poverty (and how disappointed would they be when I answered in the affirmative?) Would the Pilgrims recognize that they were part of a long heritage of exploration, now reaching out toward the edges of the solar system? The scientific method was developed in Europe just around the Pilgrims' time, the start of a period of rapid changes in politics and technology. And what would Massasoit think of how things worked out for his people?

It's easy to stand on their land in modern raingear and think romantically of their simpler time, but they certainly could not walk down the hill always assured of a meal whenever they felt like it. Nor could they predict the world as it is today. As for me, I shake off the water pooling on parts of my raingear and head back into our present, imperfect though it may be. It's finally time to leave the fog-shrouded cemetery behind and get that bowl of chili.

Where Should We Go from Here?

W hat would *I* ask, if I had the opportunity to come out of the graveyard mists above Plymouth 400 years from now? A Plymouth visitor in the year 2407 would presumably be musing over events 800 years in the past. What events from our time would be remembered 400 years from now? Will the park visitor in 2407 be wearing outlandish but warm clothes, or will he be hungry and draped in homespun of lower quality than that available in 1600? Will he be 200 years old and in better shape than I am now, or will he be 35 and dying of a bacterial infection? Will he be one of a few survivors, or one of billions of humans living both on Earth, and on other planets?

I would want to ask him whether my team won: Did science and its methods survive, or did so few people become scientists and engineers that the world could not manage its problems? People of every era must think that theirs is the critical time for humanity, but the hazards now are particularly great. We have developed incredible technologies using the scientific method – but we are not making it a high priority to train new scientists and engineers to tend what exists and make improvements where needed. Will there be enough voters who understand the tough choices (and the need to invent) we face regarding global warming and our use of energy? Science's core message is that we can always learn more: What we know will always continue to change and grow. This makes it hard to have a comfortable routine that we know will never change, but routine is a luxury in a world that is rapidly adding people.

I would like to think that the park visitor in 2407 *will* be 200 years old, and just back from a vacation on Mars. I would like to think that he will be clothed in a fuchsia and green leisure suit (hey, the future can't be *too* perfect) that was not made by people living in poverty. And I would like to think that it will still be misty and cool in Cape Cod in the summer, and that Plymouth Rock and the beach walked by Bradford and Massasoit will not lie many feet below a risen sea.

Choices

We all have choices. You chose to buy this book, for instance, presumably because you wanted to know what scientists actually do. You now know why some scientists entered their fields and what their days are like; what it means to develop a hypothesis and test it; and some of the lines between science fiction and science fact. You understand why you have to evaluate sources carefully, and you can think about how much evidence you will need to prove your points.

As for me, I chose to write this book because I saw there are not a lot of ways for people who are not regularly exposed to scientists to understand what they do and, more so, what motivates them. No one likes rapid change, and many of us, consciously or otherwise, blame science for moving the world too fast. Not doing anything when the world still needs a lot of help in a lot of areas is a choice, too – and perhaps no longer the best one to make, in many circumstances. All of us have the ability to read, to vote and to support science in small ways. When you hear an attack on science or scientists, use the factors laid out in this book to determine what arguments are based on reality and evidence, rather than politics and wishful thinking – and make your hypothesis heard!

All of us – scientists, students, citizens – have in our hands whether the visitor to Plymouth in 2407 has to arrive by boat, and whether he has the resources to do more than survive. Think about what has made the changes since 1620 possible and consider: What is the best way to honor those long-ago Plymouth residents, and the many scientists and other world-changers who have come along since then? The best way is to become a bit of an explorer – a part-time scientist – yourself.

There are plenty of questions left to ask! Get out there and ask them until you believe the answers.

Resources

Where to Learn More

Throughout this book I've urged you to look carefully at what you read and to get as close to a scientific source as you can. The list of suggested sources here is not meant to include everything that is out there at the moment. It will, however, get you started!

Some of the magazines aimed at scientists themselves (usually referred to as *journals*) require a rather expensive subscription. However, many journals have websites that allow anyone to view a summary – called an *abstract* – of articles in the journal. Sometimes the abstract is enough for an overview of an issue, if, for example, you see something about a topic in the popular press or on TV and you suspect the coverage is not accurate. Sometimes you can purchase the entire article in question for a few dollars; or you might read the abstract and get some ideas of other words to use to continue researching. Once you know names of some authors of papers on the topic, perhaps where they work, and some other words that are relevant, you can then do an internet search on those name(s) and other related words and find more background that way, perhaps by bringing up the scientist's own website.

For scientists in general, two weekly journals are *Science,* published by the American Association for the

Advancement of Science (AAAS, www.aaas.org), and *Nature*, published in Britain and somewhat more international in scope. Both require a subscription, but post online some articles of general public or policy interest for free. The website for *Science* is www.sciencemag .org and *Nature* can be found at www.nature.com/ nature. *Nature* and *Science* also have excellent associated podcasts, which are a great way to keep up with what's going on. You can search for them under "science" in your favorite podcast subscription tool. Speaking of podcasts, scientists at Cambridge University in England produce a wonderful website and very informative yet entertaining podcast, *The Naked Scientists*. Their website, www.thenakedscientists.com, links you to the various ways of listening to their podcast and also supplies fun experiments to try at home.

The National Academy of Sciences has a website, www.nationalacademies.org, with position papers available for free download on a variety of topics. The academy website has quite a few books available for free download, as well as the journal *PNAS (Proceedings of the National Academy of Sciences)*, available at www.pnas.org. If you are interested in science and public policy, the Union of Concerned Scientists website at www.ucsusa.org is also a good resource. At the moment it is focused mainly on global warming, but other topics are covered as well. For medical news, the

Journal of the American Medical Association (JAMA) is available online at jama.ama-assn.org and the *New England Journal of Medicine* at content.nejm.org. Both require subscriptions for full access, but, like *Science* and *Nature*, have some content of broad interest available for free.

For magazines more aimed at the general public, I would suggest *Scientific American* (www.sciam.com), *New Scientist* (www.newscientist.com) and *Science News* (www.sciencenews.org) as publications that are consistently excellent and cover a variety of topics. Some content is available online for free.

A great deal of material is available about the evolution discussion. A good central source for scientifically validated points of view is the National Center for Science Education (www.ncseweb.org). For materials on the discussion and how it relates to religion, some eloquent materials can be found by searching for "George Coyne evolution" to locate points of view expressed by Coyne, a Catholic priest and formerly director of the Vatican's astronomical observatory. As I noted in Section 5, I have found his down-to-earth discussions good background for developing my own thoughts on this topic.

The National Science Teachers Association (NSTA) has many resources and links available on its website, www.nsta.org. Its online store sells a variety of general-interest books about how to teach science effectively. Scientists' blogs also contain good, if less formal, discussions about issues of the day. For example, the website www.badastronomy.com has some good discussion debunking myths and pseudoscience, such as astrology. The Skeptics Society (www.skeptic.com) also has a lot of great resources to help you separate things that sound good from things that have actually been examined scientifically.

Who are some good authors if you want to learn some science but don't necessarily want to read textbooks? Simon Winchester has written terrific stories about how various geological events (like the San Francisco earthquake and the eruption of the Krakatoa volcano) have affected both scientists and the public. John McPhee writes lyrical essays about how geologists do their work and the implications of local geology for people who live in the areas studied. Paleontologist Stephen Jay Gould and astronomer Carl Sagan wrote broadly on the nature of science as well as focusing on their respective areas of expertise. If you're interested in how engineers design things, Henry Petroski has written several books, notably *To Engineer Is Human: The Role of Failure in Successful Design* and *The Evolution of Useful Things: How Everyday Artifacts – from Forks and Pins to Paper Clips and Zippers – Came to Be as They Are,* that give many examples of how even simple things needed an inventor and an "aha" moment to come into being.

And last but not least, get out there to see and hear scientists in person. If you live in a city with a university, see whether there's a public lecture series that includes scientists – and if you go to a lecture, don't hesitate to ask a question!

189

About the Author